THE ESSENTIAL GUIDE TO
SELF-SUFFICIENT LIVING

THE ESSENTIAL GUIDE TO
SELF-SUFFICIENT LIVING

Vegetable Gardening, Canning and Fermenting, Keeping Chickens, and More

ABIGAIL R. GEHRING
EDITOR OF *BACK TO BASICS*

Good Books

New York, New York

Some of the material in this book appeared first in *Good Living Guide to Country Skills*.

Some of the material in the Canning section (starting on page 91) is from the National Center for Home Food Preservation.

Good Books books may be purchased in bulk at special discounts for sales promotion, corporate gifts, fund-raising, or educational purposes. Special editions can also be created to specifications. For details, contact the Special Sales Department, Good Books, 307 West 36th Street, 11th Floor, New York, NY 10018 or info@skyhorsepublishing.com.

Good Books is an imprint of Skyhorse Publishing, Inc.®, a Delaware corporation.

Visit our website at www.goodbooks.com.

10 9 8 7 6

Library of Congress Cataloging-in-Publication Data is available on file.

Cover design by Daniel Brount
Cover images courtesy of Shutterstock.com

Print ISBN: 978-1-68099-711-8
Ebook ISBN: 978-1-5107-6419-4

Photos on pages 5, 6, 8–9, 47, and 170 by Abigail Gehring
Illustration on page 70 by Tim Lawrence
Remaining photos courtesy of Shutterstock.com.

Printed in China

Contents

Growing Things

Choosing a Site for Your Garden

When starting a new garden bed on a plot that hasn't recently been cultivated, I recommend starting small. After the first growing season—once you've seen how well things grow in the soil and have a sense of how much time it takes to maintain the garden—you can certainly expand if you choose to. A garden that is about 25 feet squared can provide plenty of vegetables for a small family if it's well planned and well tended.

Keep the following in mind as you pick a spot:

1. Sunlight
Your plants will do best with at least 6 hours of direct sunlight per day, so look for a spot that is far enough away from the shade of trees, shrubs, houses, or hillsides. Certain vegetables, such as broccoli and spinach, grow just fine in shadier spots, so if your garden does receive some shade, plant those types of vegetables in the shadier areas.

2. Proximity
If your property allows, having your garden a short walking distance from your home will make it easier for you to tend to it and to run out and grab vegetables or herbs for a meal.

3. Soil Quality

You do not need perfect soil to start and grow a productive garden, but your plants will certainly do better if the soil is fertile, full of organic materials that provide nutrients to the plant roots, and easy to dig and till. Loose, well-drained soil is ideal. If there is a section of your yard where water does not easily drain after a good, soaking rain, try to avoid that area. Furthermore, soils that are of a clay or sandy consistency are not as effective for growing plants. Most soil will need some attention before you plant seeds or seedlings, and some gardens take 2 or 3 years of attention before the soil is ready to give your plants the nutrients they need to thrive.

See page 19 for tips on improving your soil.

TIP

Don't plant anything too close to a tree. The tree will hog the soil's nutrients and the sunlight.

4. Water Availability

A successful garden needs around 1 inch of water per week to thrive. Situating your garden near a spigot or hose will allow you to keep the soil moist and your plants happy during dry periods.

5. Elevation

Avoid situating your garden in a low-lying area, such as at the base of a slope, where cold air collects. Lower areas do not warm as quickly in the spring, and frost forms quickly during the spring and fall.

Your garden should, if at all possible, be elevated slightly, on ground that is higher up.

Flowers That Do Well in Partial and Full Shade

- Bee balm
- Bellflower
- Bleeding heart
- Cardinal flower
- Coleus
- Columbine
- Daylily
- Dichondra
- Fern
- Forget-me-not
- Globe daisy
- Golden bleeding heart
- Impatiens
- Leopardbane
- Lily of the valley
- Meadow rue
- Pansy
- Periwinkle
- Persian violet
- Primrose
- Rue anemone
- Snapdragon
- Sweet alyssum
- Thyme

Vegetables That Can Grow in Partial Shade

- Arugula
- Beans
- Beets
- Broccoli
- Brussels sprouts
- Cauliflower
- Endive
- Kale
- Leaf lettuce
- Peas
- Radishes
- Spinach
- Swiss chard

Tips for Gardening on a Small Plot

1) **Grow up.** Vining crops, such as tomatoes, pole beans, peas, and cucumbers, can be grown vertically on trellises, fences, or stakes.
2) **Window boxes.** Herbs, salad greens, and strawberries can be grown in window boxes.
3) **Choose wisely.** Plant veggies with high yields for the amount of space they take, such as radishes, lettuce, carrots, garlic, onions, and spinach.

Companion Planting

Plants have natural substances built into their structures that repel or attract certain insects and can have an effect on the growth rate and even the flavor of the other plants around them. Thus, some plants aid each other's growth when planted in close proximity and others inhibit each other. Smart companion planting will help your garden remain healthy, beautiful, and in harmony, while deterring certain insect pests and other factors that could be potentially detrimental to your garden plants.

The charts on the following pages list various types of garden vegetables, herbs, and flowers and their respective companion and "enemy" plants.

The Native Americans grew pumpkins, corn (maize), and pole beans close together. Called "The Three Sisters," they're a perfect team—the corn provides "poles" for the beans to climb, the beans add nitrogen to the soil, which helps the other plants, and the foliage from the pumpkins helps the soil retain moisture. The prickly hairs on the pumpkin vines also help to deter pests.

See page 40 for more ways to rid your garden of unwanted pests.

Vegetables

Type	Companion Plant(s)	Avoid
Asparagus	Tomatoes, parsley, basil	Onions, garlic, potatoes
Beans	Eggplant	Tomatoes, onions, kale
Beets	Mint	Runner beans
Broccoli	Onions, garlic, leeks	Tomatoes, peppers, mustard
Cabbage	Onions, garlic, leeks	Tomatoes, peppers, beans
Carrots	Leeks, beans	Radishes
Celery	Daisies, snapdragons	Corn, aster flower
Corn	Legumes, squash, cucumber	Tomatoes, celery
Cucumber	Radishes, beets, carrots	Tomatoes
Eggplant	Marigolds, mint	Runner beans
Leeks	Carrots	Legumes
Lettuce	Radishes, carrots	Celery, cabbage, parsley
Melon	Pumpkin, squash	None
Peppers	Tomatoes	Beans, cabbage, kale
Onions	Carrots	Peas, beans
Peas	Beans, corn	Onions, garlic
Potatoes	Horseradish	Tomatoes, cucumber
Tomatoes	Carrots, celery, parsley	Corn, peas, potatoes, kale

Herbs

Type	Companion Plant(s)	Avoid
Basil	Chamomile, anise	Sage
Chamomile	Basil, cabbage	Other herbs
Cilantro	Beans, peas	None
Chives	Carrots	Peas, beans
Dill	Cabbage, cucumber	Tomatoes, carrots
Fennel	Dill	Everything else
Garlic	Cucumber, peas, lettuce	None
Oregano	Basil, peppers	None
Peppermint	Broccoli, cabbage	None
Rosemary	Sage, beans, carrots	None
Sage	Rosemary, beans	None
Summer savory	Onions, green beans	None

Flowers

Type	Companion Plant(s)	Avoid
Geraniums	Roses, tomatoes	None
Marigolds	Tomatoes, peppers	None
Petunias	Squash, asparagus	None
Sunflowers	Corn, tomatoes	None
Tansies	Roses, cucumber, squash	None

TIP

Hedgehogs love eating slugs and snails, making them excellent guests in your garden. If possible, leave a small area near your garden wild, which will encourage hedgehogs to hang out where you need them most. You can even purchase or build and install a little shelter in a shady spot near your garden for hedgehogs to camp out in. Never use slug pellets or other chemicals to kill slugs, since they'll also kill the hedgehogs (when they eat the dead slugs).

Improving Your Soil

It can take a few years to nurture your soil to a point where it's able to support a thriving vegetable garden. You may get lucky and find that your veggies sprout up strong and healthy and continue to grow through the season, but if not, don't despair. Most soil needs a little help in the form of compost or other organic fertilizers.

Composting

Composting is nature's own way of recycling yard and household wastes by converting them into valuable fertilizer, soil organic matter, and a source of plant nutrients. The result of this controlled decomposition of organic matter—a dark, crumbly, earthy-smelling material—works wonders on all kinds of soil by providing vital nutrients and contributing to good aeration and moisture-holding capacity, to help plants grow and look better.

Composting can be very simple or very involved, depending on how much yard waste you have, how fast you want results, and the effort you are willing to invest. Because all organic matter eventually decomposes, composting speeds up the process by providing an ideal environment for bacteria and other decomposing microorganisms. The composting season

coincides with the growing season, when conditions are favorable for plant growth, so those same conditions work well for biological activity in the compost pile. However, since compost generates heat, the process may continue later into the fall or winter. The final product—called humus or compost—looks and feels like fertile garden soil.

What to Compost

- Cardboard
- Coffee grounds
- Corn cobs
- Corn stalks
- Food scraps
- Grass clippings
- Hedge trimmings
- Livestock manure
- Newspapers
- Plant stalks
- Pine needles
- Old potting soil
- Sawdust
- Seaweed
- Shredded paper
- Straw
- Tea bags
- Telephone books
- Tree leaves and twigs
- Vegetable scraps
- Weeds without seed heads
- Wood chips
- Woody brush

What NOT to Compost

- Bread and grains
- Cooking oil
- Dairy products
- Dead animals
- Diseased plant material
- Dog or cat manure
- Grease or oily foods
- Meat or fish scraps
- Noxious or invasive weeds
- Weeds with seed heads

There are four basic ingredients for composting: nitrogen, carbon, water, and air. A wide range of materials may be composted because anything that was once alive will naturally decompose. The starting materials for composting, commonly referred to as feedstocks, include leaves, grass clippings, straw, vegetable and fruit scraps, coffee grounds, livestock manure, sawdust, and shredded paper. However, some materials that should always be avoided include diseased plants, dead animals, noxious weeds, meat scraps that may attract animals, and dog or cat manure, which can carry disease. Since adding kitchen wastes to compost may attract flies and insects, make a hole in the center of your pile and bury the waste.

For best results, you want a ratio of about 30 parts carbon to 1 part nitrogen. Carbon ingredients are the brown, or dry, ingredients—dry leaves, sawdust, straw, wood chips, corn stalks, cardboard, and peanut shells. Nitrogen ingredients are the green, or wet, things—vegetable scraps, weeds, grass clippings, and coffee grounds (even though they're not green, hopefully!). A very basic compost pile involves layering or mixing a small amount of grass clippings and vegetable scraps (nitrogen), for example, with lots of dried leaves and twigs (carbon) in a pile or enclosure.

Though rain provides the moisture, you may need to water the pile in dry weather or cover it in extremely wet weather. The microorganisms, which are small forms of plant and animal life, in the compost pile function best when the materials are as damp as a wrung-out sponge—not saturated with water. A moisture content of 40 to 60 percent is preferable. To test for adequate moisture, reach into your compost pile, grab a handful of material, and squeeze it. If a few drops of water come out, it probably has enough moisture. If it doesn't, add water by putting a hose into the pile so that you aren't just wetting the top, or, better yet, water the pile as you turn it.

Air is the only part that cannot be added in excess. For proper aeration, you'll need to punch holes in the pile so it has many air passages. The air in the pile is usually used up faster than the moisture, and extremes of sun or rain can adversely affect this balance, so the materials must be turned or mixed up often with a pitchfork, rake, or other garden tool to add air that will sustain high temperatures, control odor, and yield faster decomposition. Over time, you'll see that the microorganisms will break down the organic material. Bacteria are the first to break down plant tissue and are the most numerous and effective compost makers in your compost pile. Fungi and protozoans soon join the bacteria and, later in the cycle, centipedes, millipedes, beetles, sow bugs, nematodes, worms, and numerous others complete the composting process.

Apply finished compost to your garden bed in the spring before you start to plant. If it's a new garden bed, apply 4 to 6 inches of compost. If it's a well-established garden bed with healthy soil, just a few inches should be fine. You can also add partially finished compost to the garden bed in the fall and allow it to finish decomposing over the winter. You can also cover the garden with fallen leaves in the autumn for extra nitrogen. Either way, in the spring, till the layer of compost and/or leaves into the existing soil, mixing them together before raking the garden smooth for planting.

Speedy Compost

Typically, a compost pile needs to sit for 6 to 12 months before it's ready to spread on a garden, but it's possible to make compost in just a couple of weeks. Shredding materials before adding them to the compost pile will move the process along significantly. You can use a chipper or shredder, or use pruning sheers to cut everything into small pieces. Keeping the 30:1 ratio of carbon to nitrogen will also speed up the decomposition process. Place a piece of old carpet or a tarp over your compost pile to help hold in the heat, and turn the compost every 2 days to increase air flow.

Seven Steps to Compost

1. Choose a level, well-drained site, preferably near your garden. Decide whether you will be using a bin, making a crate out of wood pallets or

scrap wood, or just making a pile on the ground. In urban areas, there may be regulations requiring rodent-proof bins.

2. Ideally, your pile should be at least 3 feet by 3 feet, and no taller than 5 feet, as not enough air will reach the microorganisms at the center if it is too tall. When composting is completed, the total volume of the original materials is usually reduced by 30 to 50 percent.

3. Build your pile by alternating layers of high-carbon and high-nitrogen material.

4. Keep the pile moist but not wet. Soggy piles encourage the growth of organisms that can live without oxygen and cause unpleasant odors.

5. Punch holes in the sides of the pile for aeration. The pile will heat up and then begin to cool. The most efficient decomposing bacteria thrive in temperatures between 110 and 160°F. You can track this with a compost thermometer, or you can simply reach into the pile to determine if it is uncomfortably hot to the touch.

6. Check your bin regularly during the composting season to ensure optimum moisture and aeration are present in the material being composted.

7. Move materials from the center to the outside of the pile and vice versa. Turn every couple of days for speedy compost, or less frequently if you're not in a rush. Finished compost will smell sweet and be cool and crumbly to the touch.

The "No-Turn" Method

You can continue to add kitchen scraps, weeds, lawn clippings, and other compostable materials to your pile after the pile is built, though it will slow down the composting process. For kitchen scraps, dig a little hole in the pile, place the scraps inside, and cover it with dried leaves or other carbon-rich materials. With the "no-turn" method, you can just continue adding to the pile without mixing or stirring it up. This method will take several months to a year to achieve finished compost, but it's easy and allows you to continue adding materials to the top part of the pile. When the materials at the bottom of the pile have decomposed, you can dig the soil out and use it on your garden beds.

Q & A

Q: We have access to livestock manure. Should we use it on our garden beds? How?

A: Manure from horses, cows, sheep, rabbits, llamas, goats, hamsters, or chickens can be added to your compost. Waste from meat-eating animals—dogs, cats, lizards, etc.—should not be added to your compost, as it may contain harmful bacteria. Composting manure, rather than adding it directly to garden beds as a fertilizer, reduces the risk of pathogens contaminating your vegetables. Fresh manure can also dehydrate your plants. So throw it on that compost pile and give it a mix! Or you can compost the manure in its own separate pile, which takes about six months. Or spread fresh manure on your garden bed in the fall and allow it to compost over the winter months. Oftentimes, livestock manure is already mixed with hay or straw from the animals' bedding. If not, be sure to add plenty of carbon-rich materials along with the manure.

Vermicomposting

Vermicomposting uses worms to compost. This takes up very little space and can be done year-round in a basement or garage. It is an excellent way to dispose of kitchen wastes. Here's how to make your own vermicomposting pile:

1. Obtain a plastic storage bin. One bin measuring 1 foot by 2 feet by 3½ feet will be enough to meet the needs of a family of six.
2. Drill eight to ten holes about ¼ inch in diameter in the bottom of the bin for drainage.
3. Line the bottom of the bin with a fine nylon mesh to keep the worms from escaping.
4. Put a tray underneath to catch the drainage.
5. Rip newspaper into pieces to use as bedding and pour water over the strips until they are thoroughly moist. Place these shredded bits on one side of your bin. Do not let them dry out.
6. Add worms to your bin. It's best to have about 2 pounds of worms (roughly two thousand worms) per 1 pound of food waste. You may want to start with less food waste and increase the amount as your worm population grows. Redworms are recommended for best

composting, but other species can be used. Redworms are the common, small worms found in most gardens and lawns. You can collect them from under a pile of mulch or order them from a garden catalog.

7. Provide worms with food waste such as vegetable peelings. Do not add fat or meat products. Limit their feed, as too much at once may cause the material to rot.
8. Keep the bin in a dark location away from extreme temperatures.
9. Wait about 3 months and you'll see that the worms have changed the bedding and food waste into compost. At this time, open your bin in a bright light and the worms will burrow into the bedding. Add fresh bedding and more food to the other side of the bin. The worms should migrate to the new food supply.
10. Scoop out the finished compost and apply to your plants or save to use in the spring.

Cover Crops and Green Manure

Some plants help to improve soil while they're growing by adding nitrogen, suppressing weeds, and reducing pests. These "cover crops" can then be tilled into the soil, becoming "green manure." The plants act as compost right in the garden bed, returning nutrients to the soil as they decompose. Cover crops are best for areas with longer growing seasons, but can be used in cooler climates with the right planning.

Summer cover crops should be fast-growing plants that can be grown, cut just before they flower, wilted, and turned under the soil before it's time to plant your vegetable garden, or between crops. A winter cover crop is planted after the summer growing season and left to cover the ground over the winter. Legumes are particularly helpful in fixing atmospheric nitrogen in the soil. In cool climates, hardy crops such as hairy vetch or rye make good winter cover crops. For summer cover crops (or for winter cover crops in more temperate climates), crimson clover is excellent.

To plant a cover crop, clear the area of any rocks or other debris, till the soil, rake it smooth, and scatter the seeds evenly over the prepared soil (check seed packets to determine how thickly seeds should be scattered). Use a rake to cover the seeds with

Worms eat twice their body weight every day! Earthworms don't have eyes or ears, but one end of their bodies is more sensitive to light than the other.

soil and then use a hose to lightly mist the area. The crop should not require much attention until it's just about to flower or the seed heads have just emerged. At that point, for summer cover crops, mow down the plants, allow them to dry for several days, and then till them under the soil. Let the crop decompose for 2 to 3 weeks before planting your vegetable crop. Winter cover crops can simply be left until spring, when they can be cut down and tilled under.

Crimson clover covering a small field.

Growing Vegetables and Herbs

Once you've chosen a spot for your garden (as well as the size you want to make your garden bed) and prepared the soil with compost or other fertilizer, it's time to start planting. Read the instructions on the back of the seed package or on the plastic tag in your seedling pot to determine how closely the seeds or seedlings should be planted and how deep they should be.

Before planting, smooth the soil out with a rake. To create straight rows, pull a string taut from one side of the garden to the other, securing it a few inches above the ground with garden stakes or twigs. Then use a hoe to create a small trench along the string's shadow on the soil. Place the seeds in the trench according to the directions on the seed packet, cover with soil, pat down gently, and then mist the soil with a garden hose.

Corn plants sprouting in a row.

Along with your vegetables, you'll find weeds sprouting up. These should be pulled up and tossed into your compost pile so that they don't compete with your vegetables for sunlight and nutrients.

Seedlings

If you live in a cooler region with a shorter growing period, you will want to start some of your plants indoors. To do this, obtain plug flats (trays separated into many small cups or "cells") or make your own small planters by poking holes in the bottom of paper cups. Fill the cups two-thirds full with potting soil or composted soil. Bury the seeds at the recommended depth, according to the instructions on the package.

Tamp down the soil lightly and water. Keep the seedlings in a warm, well-lit place, such as the kitchen, to encourage germination. Covering the cups with plastic wrap can help speed up the seed germination; just be sure to remove the plastic as soon as you see any seedlings poking through the dirt. Once the weather begins to warm up and you are fairly certain you won't be getting any more frosts (you can contact your local extension office to find out the last "frost-free" date for your area) you can begin to acclimate your seedlings to the great outdoors.

First place them in a partially shady spot outdoors that is protected from strong wind. After a couple of days, move them into direct sunlight, and then finally transplant them to the garden.

TIP

Got milk? Use it to fertilize your garden. If your milk is starting to go bad, don't pour it down the drain! Mix it with an equal amount of water and pour around the base of your plants, or spray onto plants' leaves. The calcium will help to prevent blossom-end rot, which can occur in squash, tomatoes, and peppers, and powdery mildew, which can show up on the leaves of almost any plant.

Plants to Start Indoors		
Crop	**Weeks before transplanting**	**Seed planting depth**
Broccoli	4–6	¼–½ in.
Cabbage	4–6	¼–½ in.
Cucumber	4–5	½ in.
Eggplant	8	¼ in.
Herbs	4	¼ in.
Lettuce	4–5	¼ in.
Melon	4–5	¼ in.
Onions	8	¼ in.
Peppers	8	¼ in.
Pumpkin	2–4	1 in.
Summer squash	2–4	¾–1 in.
Tomatoes	8	¼ in.
Watermelon	4–5	½–¾ in.
Winter squash	2–4	1 in.

TIP

Many vegetables can be grown from food scraps. Lettuce, celery, and fennel can be regrown by saving the base of the vegetable and placing it in a shallow container with a little warm water. Place in a sunny spot and watch the leaves or stalks begin to grow.

Tomato plant seedlings, ready to transplant into the garden.

Mulching

Mulch is simply a protective layer of material that is spread on top of the soil to enrich the soil, prevent weed growth, and help provide a better growing environment for your garden plants and flowers. Mulches can be either organic—such as grass clippings, bark chips, compost, ground corn cobs, chopped corn stalks, leaves, manure, newspaper, peanut shells, peat moss, pine needles, sawdust, straw, and wood shavings—or inorganic—such as stones, brick chips, and plastic. Both organic and inorganic mulches have numerous benefits, including:

1. Protecting the soil from erosion
2. Reducing compaction from the impact of heavy rains
3. Conserving moisture, thus reducing the need for frequent watering
4. Maintaining a more even soil temperature
5. Preventing weed growth
6. Keeping fruits and vegetables clean
7. Keeping feet clean and allowing access to the garden even when it's damp
8. Providing a "finished" look to the garden

Organic mulches also have the benefit of improving the condition of the soil. As these mulches slowly decompose, they provide organic matter to help keep the soil loose. This improves root growth, increases the infiltration of water, improves the water-holding capacity of the soil, provides a source of plant nutrients, and establishes an ideal environment for earthworms and other beneficial soil organisms.

Add mulch around your plants once they're a couple inches tall. Spread bark mulch and wood chips 2 to 4 inches deep, keeping it an inch or two away from tree trunks. Scatter chopped and composted leaves 3 to 4 inches deep. If using dry leaves,

Adding wood chips around seedlings helps to prevent weeds from popping up.

apply about 6 inches deep. Grass clippings, if spread too thick, tend to compact and rot, becoming slimy and smelly. They should be applied 2 to 3 inches deep, and additional layers should be added as clippings decompose. Make sure not to use clippings from lawns treated with herbicides. Sheets of newspaper should be only ¼ inch thick and covered lightly with grass clippings or other mulch material to anchor them. If other mulch materials are not available, cover the edges of the newspaper with soil. If using compost, apply 3 to 4 inches deep.

Organic Mulching Materials

Bark chips	Hay	Pine needles
Chopped corn	Leaves	Sawdust
stalks	Manure	Straw
Compost	Newspaper	Wood shavings
Grass clippings	Peanut shells	
Ground corn cobs	Peat moss	

Container Gardening

If you have limited yard space or a particularly short growing season, planting in containers may be the way to go. While the amount that can be grown in a container is certainly limited, container gardens work well for tomatoes, peppers, cucumbers, herbs, salad greens, and many flowering annuals. Choose vegetable varieties that have been specifically bred for container growing. You can obtain this information online or at your garden center.

A container garden can be placed anywhere—on the patio, balcony, rooftop, or windowsill. Container gardening also brings birds and butterflies right to your doorstep. Hanging baskets of fuchsia or pots of snapdragons are frequently visited by hummingbirds, allowing for up-close observation.

1. Choose a sunny area for your container plants. Your plants will need at least 5 to 6 hours of sunlight a day. Some plants, such as cucumbers, may need more. Select plants that are suitable for container growing. Usually their name will have words such as "patio," "bush," "dwarf," "toy," or "miniature" in them. Peppers, onions, carrots, most herbs, and many flowers are also good choices.
2. Choose a planter that is at least 5 gallons, unless the plant is very small. Poke holes in the bottom if they don't already exist; the soil must be able to drain to prevent the roots from rotting. Avoid terra-cotta or dark-colored pots, as they tend to dry out quickly.
3. Fill your container with potting soil. Good potting soil will have a mixture of peat moss and vermiculite. You can make your own potting soil using composted soil. Read the directions on the seed packet or label to determine how deep to plant your seeds.
4. Check the moisture of the soil frequently. You don't want the soil to become muddy, but the soil should always feel damp to the touch. Do not wait until the plant is wilting to water it—at that point, it may be too late.

Herbs grow well in pots and can easily be brought inside and placed near a sunny window during the winter months.

Tips for Growing Herbs in Pots

- Growing several kinds of herbs together helps the plants to thrive. A few exceptions to this rule are oregano, lemon balm, and tea balm. These herbs should be planted on their own because they will overtake the other herbs in your container.
- You may wish to choose your herbs according to color to create attractive arrangements for your home. Any of the following herbs will grow well in containers:
  - Silver herbs: artemisias, curry plants, santolinas
  - Golden herbs: lemon thyme, calendula, nasturtium, sage, lemon balm
  - Blue herbs: borage, hyssop, rosemary, catnip
  - Green herbs: basil, mint, marjoram, thyme, parsley, chives, tarragon
  - Pink and purple herbs: oregano (the flowers are pink), lavender
- If you decide to transplant your herbs in the summer months, they will grow quite well outdoors and will give you a larger harvest.

TIP

Epsom salt can help your tomatoes and peppers grow better and produce tastier veggies, whether in a container or a regular garden bed. Epsom salt is high in magnesium, a nutrient tomatoes and peppers are often lacking. When planting the seedlings, dig a small hole and place about 1 tablespoon of Epsom salt at the bottom. Cover with a layer of soil, insert the seedlings, and tamp down the earth around the plant. Every 2 weeks, water the plants with a solution of 1 tablespoon of Epsom salt in a gallon of tepid water.

A raised bed with hoops can easily be converted to a greenhouse during the colder months.

Raised Beds

A raised bed creates an ideal environment for growing, since the soil concentration can be closely monitored and, as it is raised above the ground, it reduces the compaction of plants from people walking on the soil.

Raised beds are typically 2 to 6 feet wide and as long as needed. In most cases, a raised bed consists of a "frame" that is filled in with nutrient-rich soil (including compost or organic fertilizers) and is then planted with a variety of vegetables or flowers, depending on the gardener's preference. By controlling the bed's construction and the soil mixture that goes into the bed, a gardener can effectively reduce the amount of weeds that will grow in the garden.

TIP

You can convert your raised bed into a greenhouse. Just add hoops to your bed by bending PVC pipes (using a heat gun) and connecting them to the bed. Then, clip greenhouse plastic to the PVC pipes, and you have your own greenhouse.

When planting seeds or young sprouts in a raised bed, it is best to space the plants equally distant from each other on all sides. This will ensure that the leaves will be touching once the plant is mature, thus saving space and reducing the soil's moisture loss.

Plan Out Your Raised Bed

1. Think about how you'd like your raised bed to look, and then design the shape. You can build a simple rectangular frame or you can create a raised bed in the shape of a circle, hexagon, or star. Just keep in mind that you'll want to be able to reach all plants in the garden without stepping up onto the garden bed, so narrow raised beds usually make the most sense. The main purpose of this box is to hold soil.

2. Make a drawing of your raised bed, measure your available garden space, and add those measurements to your drawing. This will allow you to determine how much material is needed. Generally, your bed should be at least 24 inches in height.

3. Decide what kind of material you want to use for your raised bed. You can use lumber, wooden pallets, synthetic wood, railroad ties, bricks, rocks, or a number of other items to hold the dirt. Using lumber is the easiest and most efficient method.

4. Make sure your bed will be situated in a place that gets plenty of sunlight. Carefully assess your placement, as your raised bed will be fairly permanent.

5. Connect the sides of your bed together (with either screws or nails) to form the desired shape of your bed. If you are using lumber, you can use 4-by-4-inch posts to serve as the corners of your bed, and then nail or screw the sides to these corner posts. By doing so, you will increase the strength of the structure and ensure that the dirt will stay inside.

6. Cover the bottom of the bed with pieces of cardboard. This will significantly reduce the number of weeds growing in your garden. Then, add some compost and then layer potting soil on top of the compost. If you have soil from other parts of your yard, feel free to use that in addition to the compost and potting soil. Plan to fill at least 1/3 of your raised bed with compost or composted manure.

7. Mix in dry organic fertilizers (like wood ash, bonemeal, and blood meal) while building your bed. Follow the package instructions for how best to mix it in.

8. Plant your garden! Raised beds are excellent choices for salad greens, carrots, onions, radishes, beets, and other root crops.

Insects and Mites

Insects damage plants in several ways. The most visible damage caused by insects is chewed plant leaves and flowers. Many pests are visible and can be readily identified, including the Japanese beetle, the Colorado potato beetle, and numerous species of caterpillars such as tent caterpillars and tomato hornworms. Other chewing insects, however, such as cutworms (which are caterpillars), come out at night to eat and burrow into the soil during the day. These are much harder to identify but should be considered likely culprits if young plants seem to disappear overnight or are found cut off at ground level.

Sucking insects are extremely common in gardens and can be very damaging to your vegetable plants and flowers. The most known of these insects are leafhoppers, aphids, mealy bugs, thrips, and mites. These insects insert their mouthparts into the plant tissues and suck out the plant juices. They also may carry diseases that they spread from plant to plant as they move about the yard. You may suspect that these insects are present if you notice misshapen plant leaves or flower petals. Often the younger leaves will appear curled or puckered. Flowers developing from the buds may only partially develop if they've been sucked by these bugs. Look on the undersides of the leaves—that is where many insects tend to gather.

Other insects cause damage to plants by boring into stems, fruits, and leaves, possibly disrupting the plant's ability to transport water. They also create opportunities for disease organisms to attack the plants. You may suspect the presence of boring insects if you see small accumulations of sawdust-like material on plant stems or fruits. Common examples of boring insects include squash vine borers and corn borers.

TIP

To get rid of aphids, mix a little dish soap with lukewarm water in a spray bottle. Spray the diluted soap on the tops and bottoms of the leaves. Aphids have a waxy coating on their bodies that will dissolve when sprayed with the soapy water, causing them to become dehydrated and then die.

Integrated Pest Management (IPM)

It is difficult, if not impossible, to prevent all pest problems in your garden every year. If your best prevention efforts have not been entirely successful, you may need to use some control methods. Integrated pest management (IPM) relies on several techniques to keep pests at acceptable population levels. The basic principles of IPM include monitoring (scouting), determining tolerable injury levels (thresholds), and applying appropriate strategies and tactics to solve the pest issue.

Unlike other methods of pest control where pesticides are applied on a rigid schedule, IPM applies only those controls that are needed, when they are needed, to control pests that will cause more than a tolerable level of damage to the plant. Although traditional IPM does sometimes involve chemical pesticides, there are organic alternatives that are strongly recommended on page 44. Organic methods may not be as effective at killing pests, but there are environmental and health risks to using chemical pesticides.

Monitoring

Monitoring is essential for a successful IPM program. Check your plants regularly for signs of damage from insects and diseases as well as indications of adequate fertility and moisture. Early identification of potential problems is essential. There are thousands of insects in a garden, many of which are harmless or even beneficial to the plants. It is important to recognize the different stages of insect development for several reasons. The caterpillar eating your plants may be the larva of the butterfly you were trying to attract. Any small larva with six spots on its back is probably a young ladybug, a very beneficial insect.

Thresholds

It is not necessary to kill every insect, weed, or disease organism invading your garden in order to maintain the plants' health. When dealing with garden pests, there's a point where the damage caused by the pest exceeds the cost of control. In a home garden, this can be difficult to determine. What you are growing and how you intend to use it will determine how much damage you are willing to tolerate. Remember that larger plants, especially those close to harvest, can tolerate more damage than a tiny seedling. A few flea beetles on a radish seedling may warrant control, whereas numerous Japanese beetles eating the leaves of beans close to harvest may not.

Mechanical/Physical Control Strategies

Many insects can simply be removed by hand. This method is definitely preferable if only a few large insects are causing the problem. Simply remove the insect from the plant and drop it into a container of soapy water or vegetable oil. Be aware that some insects have prickly spines or excrete oily substances that can cause injury to humans. Use caution when handling unfamiliar insects. Wear gloves or remove insects with tweezers.

Many insects can be removed from plants by spraying water from a hose or sprayer. Small vacuums can also be used to suck up insects. Traps can be used effectively for some insects as well. These come in a variety of styles depending on the insect to be caught. Many traps rely on the use of pheromones—naturally occurring chemicals produced by the insects and used to attract the opposite sex during mating. They are specific to each species and, therefore, will not harm beneficial species.

One caution with traps is that they may actually draw more insects into your yard, so don't place them directly in your garden. Other traps (such as yellow and blue sticky cards) are more generic and will attract numerous species. Different insects are attracted to different colors of these traps. Sticky cards can also be used effectively to monitor insect pests.

Other Pest Controls

Diatomaceous earth, a powderlike dust made of tiny marine organisms called diatoms, can be used to reduce damage from soft-bodied insects and slugs. Just spread this material on the soil and its sharp texture will cut or irritate these soft organisms while being harmless to other organisms. Put out shallow dishes of beer to trap slugs.

Biological Controls

Biological controls are nature's way of regulating pest populations. Biological controls rely on predators and parasites to keep organisms under control. Many of our present pest problems result from the loss of predator species and other biological control factors. Some biological controls include birds and bats that eat insects. A single bat can eat up to six hundred mosquitoes an hour. Many bird species eat insect pests on trees and in the garden.

Non-toxic Pesticides

Some common, non-toxic household substances are as effective as many toxic pesticides. A few drops of dishwashing detergent mixed with water and sprayed on plants is extremely effective at controlling many soft-bodied insects, such as aphids and whiteflies. Crushed garlic mixed with water may control certain insects. A baking soda solution has been shown to help control some fungal diseases on roses.

Ladybugs are welcome additions to a garden, since they eat harmful aphids and potato beetles.

Beneficial Insects That Help Control Pest Populations	
Insect	**Pest Controlled**
Green lacewings	Aphids, mealy bugs, thrips, and spider mites
Ladybugs	Aphids and Colorado potato beetles
Praying mantises	Almost any insect
Ground beetles	Caterpillars that attack trees and shrubs
Seed head weevils and other beetles	Weeds

Natural Pest Repellants	
Pest	**Repellant**
Ants	Mint, tansy, or pennyroyal
Aphids	Mint, garlic, chives, coriander, or anise
Bean leaf beetles	Potatoes, onions, or turnips
Codling moths	Common oleander
Colorado potato bugs	Green beans, coriander, or nasturtium
Cucumber beetles	Radishes or tansy
Flea beetles	Garlic, onions, or mint
Imported cabbage worms	Mint, sage, rosemary, or hyssop
Japanese beetles	Garlic, larkspur, tansy, rue, or geranium
Leafhoppers	Geranium or petunia
Mice	Onions
Root knot nematodes	French marigolds
Slugs	Prostrate rosemary or wormwood

Natural Pest Repellants, *continued*	
Pest	**Repellant**
Spider mites	Onions, garlic, cloves, or chives
Squash bugs	Radishes, marigolds, tansy, or nasturtium
Stink bugs	Radishes
Thrips	Marigolds
Tomato hornworms	Marigolds, sage, or borage
Whiteflies	Marigolds or nasturtium

Plant Diseases

Diseases need three elements to become established in plants: the disease organism, a susceptible species, and the proper environmental conditions. Some disease organisms can live in the soil for years; other organisms are carried in infected plant material that falls to the ground. Some disease organisms are carried by insects. Good sanitation will help limit some problems with disease. Choosing resistant varieties of plants and rotating annual plants also help prevent many diseases from occurring.

Plants that have adequate, but not excessive, nutrients are better able to resist attacks from both diseases and insects. Excessive rates of nitrogen often result in extremely succulent vegetative growth and can make plants more susceptible to insect and disease problems, as well as decrease their winter hardiness. Proper watering and spacing of plants limits the spread of some diseases and provides good aeration around plants, so diseases that fester in standing water cannot multiply. Trickle irrigation, where water is applied to the soil and not the plant leaves, may be helpful.

Removal of diseased material certainly limits the spread of some diseases. It is important to clean up litter dropped from diseased plants. Prune diseased branches on trees and shrubs to allow for more air circulation. When pruning diseased trees and shrubs, disinfect your pruners between cuts with a solution of chlorine bleach to avoid spreading the disease from plant to plant. Also try to control insects that may carry diseases to your plants.

You can make your own natural fungicide by combining 5 teaspoons each of baking soda and hydrogen peroxide with a gallon of water. Spray on your infected plants. Milk diluted with water is also an effective fungicide due to the potassium phosphate in it, which boosts a plant's immune system. The more diluted the solution, the more frequently you'll need to spray the plant.

TIP

Garlic can be used as a fungicide and insecticide, but remember that it will kill the good insects (like ladybugs) as well as the bad ones. Blend together 10 cloves of garlic and 1 pint of water and then strain the mixture into a spray bottle. Spray the tops and bottoms of the affected foliage.

Harvesting Your Garden

To get the best freshness, flavor, and nutritional benefits from your garden vegetables and fruits, you have to harvest them at the appropriate time. When possible, harvest your vegetables during the cool part of the morning. If you are going to can and preserve your vegetables and fruits, do so as soon as possible. Or, if this process must be delayed, cool the vegetables in ice water or crushed ice and store them in the refrigerator.

Here are some brief guidelines for harvesting various types of common garden produce:

Asparagus—Harvest the spears when they are at least 6 to 8 inches tall by snapping or cutting them at ground level. A few spears may be harvested the second year after crowns are set out. A full harvest season will last 4 to 6 weeks during the third growing season.

Beans, snap—Harvest before the seeds develop in the pod. Beans are ready to pick if they snap easily when bent in half.

Beans, lima—Harvest when the pods first start to bulge with the enlarged seeds. Pods must still be green, not yellowish.

Broccoli—Harvest the dark green, compact cluster, or head, while the buds are shut tight, before any yellow flowers appear. Smaller side shoots will develop later, providing a continuous harvest.

See page 91 for instructions on canning your harvest.

Brussels sprouts—Harvest the lower sprouts (small heads) when they are about 1 to 1½ inches in diameter by twisting them off. Removing the lower leaves along the stem will help to hasten the plant's maturity.

Cabbage—Harvest when the heads feel hard and solid.

Cantaloupe—Harvest when the stem slips easily from the fruit with a gentle tug. Another indicator of ripeness is when the netting on the skin becomes rounded and the flesh between the netting turns from a green to a tan color.

Carrots—Harvest when the roots are ¾ to 1 inch in diameter. The largest roots generally have darker tops.

Cauliflower—When preparing to harvest, exclude sunlight when the curds (heads) are 1 to 2 inches in diameter by loosely tying the outer leaves together above the curds with a string or rubber band. This process is known as blanching. Harvest the curds when they are 4 to 6 inches in diameter but still compact, white, and smooth. The head should be ready 10 to 15 days after tying the leaves.

Collards—Harvest older, lower leaves when they reach a length of 8 to 12 inches. New leaves will grow as long as the central growing point remains, providing a continuous harvest. Whole plants may be harvested and cooked if desired.

Corn, sweet—The silks begin to turn brown and dry out as the ears mature. Check a few ears for maturity by opening the top of the ear and pressing a few kernels with your thumbnail. If the exuded liquid is milky rather than clear, the ear is ready for harvesting. Cooking a few ears is also a good way to test for maturity.

Cucumbers—Harvest when the fruits are 6 to 8 inches in length. Harvest when the color is deep green and before a yellow color appears. Pick four to five times per week to encourage continuous production. Leaving mature cucumbers on the vine will stop the production of the entire plant.

Eggplant—Harvest when the fruits are 4 to 5 inches in diameter and their color is a glossy, purplish black. The fruit is getting too ripe when the color starts to dull or become bronzed. Because the stem is woody, cut—do not pull—the fruit from the plant. A short stem should remain on each fruit.

Kale—Harvest by twisting off the outer, older leaves when they reach a length of 8 to 10 inches and are medium green in color. Heavy, dark green leaves are overripe and are likely to be tough and bitter. New leaves will grow, providing a continuous harvest.

Lettuce—Harvest the older, outer leaves from leaf lettuce as soon as they are 4 to 6 inches long. Harvest heading types when the heads are moderately firm and before seed stalks form.

Mustard—Harvest the leaves and leaf stems when they are 6 to 8 inches long; new leaves will provide a continuous harvest until they become too strong in flavor and tough in texture, due to temperature extremes.

Okra—Harvest young, tender pods when they are 2 to 3 inches long. Pick the okra at least every other day during the peak growing season. Overripe pods become woody and are too tough to eat.

Onions—Harvest when the tops fall over and begin to turn yellow. Dig up the onions and allow them to dry out in the open sun for a few days to toughen the skin. Then remove the dried soil by brushing the onions lightly. Cut the stem, leaving 2 to 3 inches attached, and store in a net-type bag in a cool, dry place.

Peas—Harvest regular peas when the pods are well rounded; edible-pod varieties should be harvested when the seeds are fully developed but still fresh and bright green. Pods are getting too old when they lose their brightness and turn light or yellowish green.

Peppers—Harvest sweet peppers with a sharp knife when the fruits are firm, crisp, and full size. Green peppers will turn red if left on the plant. Allow hot peppers to attain their bright red color and full flavor while attached to the vine; then cut them and hang them to dry.

Potatoes—Harvest the tubers when the plants begin to dry and die down. Store the tubers in a cool, high-humidity location with good ventilation, such as the basement or crawl space of your house. Avoid exposing the tubers to light, as greening, which denotes the presence of dangerous alkaloids, will occur even with small amounts of light.

Pumpkins—Harvest pumpkins and winter squash before the first frost. After the vines dry up, the fruit color darkens and the skin surface resists puncture from your thumbnail. Avoid bruising or scratching the fruit while handling it. Leave a 3- to 4-inch portion of the stem attached to the fruit and store it in a cool, dry location with good ventilation.

Radishes—Harvest when the roots are ½ to 1½ inches in diameter. The shoulders of radish roots of ten appear through the soil surface when they are mature. If left in the ground too long, the radishes will become tough and woody.

Rutabagas—Harvest when the roots are about 3 inches in diameter. The roots may be stored in the ground and used as needed, if properly mulched.

Spinach—Harvest by cutting all the leaves off at the base of the plant when they are 4 to 6 inches long. New leaves will grow, providing additional harvests.

Squash, summer—Harvest when the fruit is soft, tender, and 6 to 8 inches long. The skin color often changes to a dark, glossy green or yellow, depending on the variety. Pick every 2 to 3 days to encourage continued production.

Sweet potatoes—Harvest the roots when they are large enough for use before the first frost. Avoid bruising or scratching the potatoes during handling. Ideal storage conditions are at a temperature of 55°F and a relative humidity of 85 percent. The basement or crawl space of a house may suffice.

Swiss chard—Harvest by breaking off the developed outer leaves 1 inch above the soil. New leaves will grow, providing a continuous harvest.

Tomatoes—Harvest the fruits at the most appealing stage of ripeness, when they are bright red. The flavor is best at room temperature, but ripe fruit may be held in the refrigerator at 45 to 50°F for 7 to 10 days.

Turnips—Harvest the roots when they are 2 to 3 inches in diameter but before heavy fall frosts occur. The tops may be used as salad greens when the leaves are 3 to 5 inches long.

Watermelons—Harvest when the watermelon produces a dull thud rather than a sharp, metallic sound when thumped—this means the fruit is ripe. Other ripeness indicators are a deep yellow rather than a white color where the melon touches the ground; brown tendrils on the stem near the fruit; and a rough, slightly ridged feel to the skin surface.

Tomatoes were first cultivated in the Andes by the Aztecs and Mayans around AD 700. Tomatoes made their way to Europe in the sixteenth century. In the United States, the tomato was considered to be poisonous until the mid-nineteenth century. The story goes that in 1830 in Salem, Massachusetts, one brave man stood before a crowd and consumed a ripe tomato, despite warnings that his blood would turn to acid.

Raising Animals

Keeping Chickens

Choosing a Chicken Breed

Take the time to select chickens that are well suited for your needs. If you want chickens solely for their eggs, look for chickens that are good egg-layers. Mediterranean poultry are good for first-time chicken owners, as they are easy to care for and need only the proper food to lay many eggs. If you are looking to slaughter and eat your chickens, you will want to have heavy-bodied fowl (Asiatic poultry) to get the most meat. For chickens that lay a good number of eggs and that can also be used for meat, invest in the Wyandottes or Plymouth Rock breeds. These chickens are good sources of both eggs and meat.

Wyandottes have seven distinct breeds: Silver, White, Buff, Golden, and Black are the most common. These breeds are hardy and are very popular in the United States. They are compactly built and lay excellent, dark brown eggs. They are good sitters and their meat is perfect for broiling or roasting.

Plymouth Rock chickens have three distinct breeds: Barred, White, and Buff. They are the most popular breeds in the United States and are hardy birds that grow to a medium size. These chickens are good for laying eggs, roost well, and also provide good meat. Plymouth Rock chickens are good all-around farm chickens with their docile dispositions, hardiness, tendency to be very productive egg-layers, and good meat.

You don't need to refrigerate freshly laid eggs if you don't wash them. There's a protective coating on eggs that keeps them from spoiling for a week or so (if you plan to keep your eggs for more than a week, stick them in the fridge). We refrigerate factory-farmed eggs because they're washed before being sent out to stores.

Feeding Chickens

Chickens, like most creatures, need a balanced diet of protein, carbohydrates, vitamins, fats, minerals, and water. Chickens with plenty of access to grassy areas will find most of what they need on their own. They also love to gobble up kitchen scraps, such as carrot tops, apple peels, stale bread, etc. (see sidebar on what *not* to feed them). Just toss them in the chicken pen and they'll come and peck at them. To increase egg production, and to be sure chickens have enough feed in the winter months, supplement kitchen scraps with commercial chicken feed in the form of mash, crumbles, pellets, or scratch. Or you can make your own feed out of a combination of grains, seeds, protein-rich legumes, and a gritty substance such as bonemeal, limestone, oystershell, or granite (to aid digestion, especially in winter). The correct ratio of food for a warm, secure chicken should be 1 part protein to 4 parts carbohydrates. Do not rely too heavily on corn, as it can be overly fattening for hens; combine corn with wheat or oats for the carbohydrate portion of the feed. Clover and other green foods are also beneficial to feed your chickens. How much food your chickens will need depends on their breed, their age, the season, and how much room they have to exercise. Often it's easiest and best to leave feed available at all times in several locations within the chickens' range. This will ensure that even the lowest chickens in the pecking order get the feed they need. Note that chickens at different stages of development require different nutrients and kinds of feed. If you're bringing home chicks or hatching your own, purchase a feed mix specially formulated for baby chicks.

What NOT to Feed Your Chickens

- Avocado pits and peels
- Chocolate or candy
- Citrus
- Green potato skin
- Dry beans
- Moldy or rotten food
- Rhubarb
- Onions
- Garlic
- Anything high in fat or salt
- Meat or meat scraps

Homemade Chicken Feed

4 parts corn (or more in cold months)
3 parts oat groats
2 parts wheat
2 parts alfalfa meal or chopped hay
1 part soybean meal
2 to 3 parts dried split peas, lentils, or soybean meal
2 to 3 parts bonemeal, crushed oystershell, granite grit, or limestone
½ part cod-liver oil

You may also wish to add sunflower seeds, hulled barley, millet, kamut, amaranth seeds, quinoa, sesame seeds, flaxseeds, or kelp granules. If you find that your eggs are thin-shelled, try adding more calcium to the feed (in the form of limestone or oystershell). Store feed in a covered bucket, barrel, or other container that will not allow rodents to get into it. A plastic or galvanized bucket is good, as it will also keep mold-causing moisture out of the feed.

Housing

You will need to have a structure for your chickens to live in to protect them from predators and inclement weather, and to allow the hens a safe place to lay their eggs. Foxes, weasels, coyotes, dogs, raccoons, and even some hawks are likely to come after your chickens at some point. During the day, many people choose to let their chickens roam free or in a large fenced-in area, but at night they should return to a secure hen house. You can purchase a coop or construct one yourself—a quick search online will yield a plethora of plans. Here are some guidelines to keep in mind:

- Placing your henhouse close enough to your own home will remind you to visit it frequently to feed the chickens and to gather eggs. It is best to establish the house and yard in dry soil, away from areas in your yard that are frequently damp or moist, as this is the perfect breeding ground for poultry diseases.
- The henhouse should be well-ventilated (but free from any holes or gaps between boards), warm, protected from the cold and rain, have a few windows that allow the sunlight to shine in (especially if you live in a colder climate), and have a sound roof.
- Raising the coop off the ground about a foot with cinder blocks or some other method will impede vermin and snakes from snatching young birds and eggs. The perches in your henhouse should not be more than 2½ feet above the floor, and you should place a smooth platform under the perches to catch the droppings so they can easily be cleaned. Nesting boxes should be kept in a darker part of the house and should have ample space around them.
- A fence around the area—and even over top—the coop and chicken run is in serves as further protection. Choose wire mesh fencing with small openings (1-by-2-inch); remember that weasels can sneak through very tight spaces. You may also bury galvanized hardware cloth along the perimeter of your fence to prevent animals from burrowing under it.

If you're bringing home baby chicks or hatching them, you'll need to set up a brooder with a heat lamp, absorbent bedding such as wood shavings, lights, feeders, and waterers. You can keep the brooder in a room of your home or in a basement or garage. The area should be fairly quiet and away from other pets. Spend some time researching brooders and how to care for baby chicks before bringing them home.

The hardest part of keeping chickens may be keeping them safe from predators. It's worth investing time and resources into creating a secure environment for your flock.

Keeping Bees

Beekeeping (also known as apiculture) is one of the oldest human industries. For thousands of years, honey has been considered a highly desirable food. Beekeeping is a science and can be a very profitable occupation. It is also a wonderful hobby for many people. Keeping bees can be done almost anywhere—on a farm, in a rural or suburban area, and even in urban areas. Anywhere there are sufficient flowers from which to collect nectar, bees can thrive. Apiculture relies heavily on the natural resources of a particular location and the knowledge of the beekeeper in order to be successful. Collecting and selling honey at your local farmers' market or just to family and friends can supply you with some extra cash if you are looking to make a profit from your apiary.

Why Raise Bees?

Bees are essential in the pollination and fertilization of many fruit and seed crops. If you have a garden with many flowers or fruit plants, having bees nearby will only help your garden flourish and grow year after year. Little is more satisfying than extracting your own honey for everyday use.

How to Avoid Getting Stung

Though it takes some skill, you can learn how to avoid being stung by the bees you keep. Here are some ways you can keep your bee stings to a minimum:

1. Keep gentle bees. Having bees that, by sheer nature, are not as aggressive will reduce the number of stings you are likely to receive. Carniolan bees are one of the gentlest species, and so are the Caucasian bees introduced from Russia.
2. Obtain a good "smoker" and use it whenever you'll be handling your bees. Pumping smoke of any kind into and around the beehive will render your bees less aggressive and less likely to sting you.
3. Purchase and wear a veil. This should be made out of black bobbinet and worn over your face. Also, rubber gloves help protect your hands from stings.
4. Use a "bee escape." This device is fitted into a slot made in a board the same size as the top of the hive. Slip the board into the hive before you open it to extract the honey; it allows the worker bees to slip below it but not to return back up. So, by placing the "bee escape" into the hive the day before you want to gain access to the combs and honey, you will most likely trap all the bees under the board and leave yourself free to work with the honeycombs without fear of stings.

See page 70 for plans to build your own hive.

What Type of Hive Should I Use?

Most beekeepers would agree that the best hives have suspended, movable frames where the bees make the honeycombs, which are easy to lift out. These frames, called Langstroth frames, are the most popular kind of frame used by apiculturists in the United States. Whether you build your own beehive or purchase one, it should be built strongly and should contain accurate bee spaces and a close-fitting, rainproof roof. If you are looking to have honeycombs, you must have a hive that permits the insertion of up to eight combs.

Where Should the Hive Be Situated?

Hives and their stands should be placed in an enclosure where the bees will not be disturbed by other animals or humans and where it will be generally quiet. Hives should be placed on their own stands at least 3 feet from each other. Do not allow weeds to grow near the hives and keep the hives away from walls and fences. You, as the beekeeper, need to easily access your hive without fear of obstacles.

Swarming

Swarming is simply the migration of honeybees to a new hive and is led by the queen bee. During swarming season (the warm summer days), a beekeeper must remain very alert. If you see swarming above the hive, take great care and act calmly and quietly. You want to get the swarm into your hive, but this will be tricky. If the bees land on a nearby branch or in a basket, simply approach and then "pour" them into the hive. Keep in mind that bees will more likely inhabit a cool, shaded hive than one that is baking in the hot summer sun. Sometimes it is beneficial to try to prevent swarming, such as if you already have completely full hives. Frequently removing the new honey from the hive before swarming begins will deter the bees from swarming. Shading the hives on warm days will also help keep the bees from swarming.

Bee Pastures

Bees will fly a great distance to gather food but you should try to contain them, as well as possible, to an area within 2 miles of the beehive. Make sure they have access to many honey-producing plants that you can grow in your garden. Alfalfa, asparagus, buckwheat, chestnut, clover, catnip, mustard, raspberry, roses, and sunflowers are some of the best honey-producing plants and trees. Also make sure that your bees always have access to pure, clean water.

> Propolis is a resin from poplar and evergreen trees that bees use as a kind of glue for their hives. Propolis has many health properties for people—it's an antimicrobial, helps to heal burns, prevents cavities, and can even help halt the spread of cancer. You can purchase a "propolis trap" for your hives, a sort of grid that the bees fill up with propolis, especially as the weather gets colder. Autumn is generally the best time to harvest propolis from your hives.

Preparing Your Bees for Winter

If you live in a colder region, keeping your bees alive throughout the winter months is difficult. If your queen bee happens to die in the fall, before a young queen can be reared, your whole colony will die throughout the winter. However, the queen's death can be avoided by taking simple precautions and giving careful attention to your hive come autumn. Colonies are usually lost in the winter months due to insufficient winter food storages, faulty hive construction, lack of protection from the cold and dampness, not enough or too much ventilation, or too many older bees and not enough young ones. If you live in a region that gets a few weeks of severe weather, you may want to move your colony indoors, or at least to an area that is protected from the outside elements. But the essential components of having a colony survive through the winter season are to have a good queen; a fair ratio of healthy, young, and old bees; and a plentiful supply of food.

The hive needs to retain a liberal supply of ripened honey and a thick syrup made from white cane sugar (you should feed this to your bees early enough so they have time to take the syrup and seal it over before winter). To make this syrup, dissolve 3 pounds of granulated sugar in 1 quart of boiling water and add 1 pound of pure extracted honey. If you live in an extremely cold area, you may need up to 30 pounds of this syrup, depending on how many bees and hives you have. You can use either a top feeder or a frame feeder, which fits inside the hive in the place of a frame. Fill the frame with the syrup and place sticks or grass in it to keep the bees from drowning.

Extracting Honey

To obtain the extracted honey, you'll need to keep the honeycombs in one area of the hive or packed one above the other. Before removing the filled combs, you should allow the bees ample time to ripen and cap the honey. To uncap the comb cells, simply use a sharp knife (apiary suppliers sell knives specifically for this purpose). Then put the combs in a machine called a honey extractor to extract the honey. The honey extractor whips the honey out of the cells and allows you to replace the fairly undamaged comb into the hive to be repaired and refilled. The extracted honey runs into open buckets or vats and is left, covered with a tea towel or larger cloth, to stand for a week. It should be in a warm, dry room where no ants can reach it. Skim the honey each day until it is perfectly clear. Then you can put it into cans, jars, or bottles for selling or for your own personal use.

Making Beeswax

Beeswax from the honeycomb can be used for making candles, can be added to lotions or lip balm, and can even be used in baking. Rendering wax in boiling water is especially simple when you have only a small apiary. Collect the combs, break them into chunks, roll them into balls if you like, and put them in a muslin bag. Put the bag with the beeswax into a large stockpot and bring the water to a slow boil, making sure the bag doesn't rest on the bottom of the pot and burn. The muslin will act as a strainer for the wax. Use clean, sterilized tongs to occasionally squeeze the bag. After the wax is boiled out of the bag, remove the pot from the heat and allow it to cool. Then, remove the wax from the top of the water and then re-melt it in another pot on very low heat, so it doesn't burn. Pour the melted wax into molds lined with wax paper or plastic wrap and then cool it before using it to make other items or selling it at your local farmers' market.

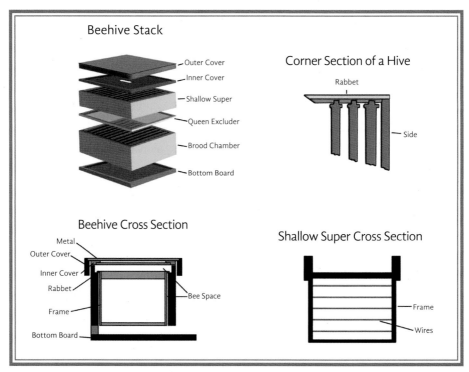

Here are some very basic plans for building your own beehive.

Keeping Goats

Goats provide us with milk and wool and thrive in arid, semitropical, and mountainous environments. In the more temperate regions of the world, goats are raised as supplementary animals, providing milk and cheese for families and acting as natural weed killers.

Breeds of Goats

Some goat breeds are small (weighing roughly 50 pounds) and some are very large (weighing up to 250 pounds). Depending on the breed, goats may have horns that are corkscrew in shape, though many domestic goats are dehorned early on to lessen any potential injuries to humans or other goats. The hair of goats can also differ—various breeds have short hair, long hair, curly hair, silky hair, or coarse hair. Goats come in a variety of colors (solid black, white, brown, or spotted).

Six Major US Goat Breeds

Alpine—Originally from Switzerland, these goats may have horns, are short haired, and are usually white and black in color. They are also good producers of milk.

Anglo-Nubian—A cross between native English goats and Indian and Nubian breeds, these goats have droopy ears, spiral horns, and short hair. They are quite tall and do best in warmer climates. They do not produce as much milk, though it is much higher in fat than other goats'. They are the most popular breed of goat in the United States.

LaMancha—A cross between Spanish Murciana and Swiss and Nubian breeds, these goats are extremely adaptable, have straight noses, have short hair, may have horns, and have very short ear pinnae. They are not as good milk producers as the Saanen and Toggenburg breeds, and their milk's fat content is much higher.

Pygmy—Originally from Africa and the Caribbean, these dwarfed goats thrive in hotter climates. For their size, they are relatively good producers of milk, though not usually considered a dairy breed.

Saanen—Originally from Switzerland, these goats are completely white, have short hair, and sometimes have horns. Goats of this breed are wonderful milk producers.

Toggenburg—Originally from Switzerland, these goats are brown with white facial, ear, and leg stripes; have straight noses; may have horns; and have short hair. This breed is very popular in the United States. These goats are good milk producers in the summer and winter seasons and survive well in both temperate and tropical climates.

Feeding Goats

Goats can sustain themselves on bushes, trees, shrubs, woody plants, weeds, briars, and herbs. Pasture is the lowest-cost feed available for goats, and allowing goats to graze in the summer months is a wonderful and economic way to keep goats, even if your yard is small. Goats thrive best when eating alfalfa or a mixture of clover and timothy. If you have a lawn and a few goats, you don't need a lawn mower if you plant these types of plants for your goats to eat. The one drawback to this is that your goats (depending on how many you own) may quickly deplete these natural resources, which can cause weed growth and erosion. Supplementing pasture feed with other foodstuff, such as greenchop, root crops, and wet brewery grains, will ensure that your yard does not become overgrazed and that your goats remain well fed and healthy. It is also beneficial to supply your goats with unlimited access to hay while they are grazing. Make sure that your goats have easy access to shaded areas and fresh water, and offer a salt-and-mineral mix on occasion.

Dry forage is another good source of feed for your goats. It is relatively inexpensive to grow or buy and consists of good-quality legume hay (alfalfa or clover). Legume hay is high in protein and has many essential minerals beneficial to your goats. Be sure that the forage had an early cutting date, which will allow for easier digestion of the nutrients. If your forage is green in color, it most likely contains more vitamin A, which is good for promoting goat health.

Goat Milk

Goat milk is a wonderful substitute for those who are unable to tolerate cow's milk, or for the elderly, babies, and those suffering from stomach ulcers. Milk from goats is also high in vitamin A and niacin but does not have the same amount of vitamins B6, B12, and C as cow's milk.

Lactating goats do need to be fed the best-quality legume hay or green forage possible, as well as grain. Give the grain to the doe at a rate that equals ½ pound grain for every pound of milk she produces.

TIP

Goats are social animals and can become depressed if kept away from other goats. If you're going to get a goat, it's a good idea to get two or three.

Common Diseases Affecting Goats

Goats tend to get more internal parasites than other herd animals. Some goats develop infectious arthritis, pneumonia, coccidiosis, scabies, liver fluke disease, and mastitis. It is a good idea to establish a relationship with a veterinarian who specializes in small farm animals to periodically check your goats for various diseases.

Milking a Goat

Milking a goat takes some practice and patience, especially when you first begin. However, once you establish a routine and rhythm to the milking, the whole process should run relatively smoothly. The main thing to remember is to keep calm and never pull on the teat, as this will hurt the goat and she might upset the milk bucket. The goat will pick up on any anxiousness or nervousness on your part and it could affect how cooperative she is during the milking.

Supplies
- A grain bucket and grain for feeding the goat while milking is taking place
- A milking stand
- A metal bucket to collect the milk
- A stool to sit on (optional)
- A warm, sterilized wipe or cloth that has been boiled in water
- Teat-dip solution (2 tablespoons bleach, 1 quart water, 1 drop normal dish detergent mixed together)

Directions
1. Ready your milking stand by filling the grain bucket with enough grain to last throughout the entire milking. Then retrieve the goat, separating her from any other goats to avoid distractions and unsuccessful milking. Place the goat's head through the head hold of the milking stand so she can eat the grain and then close the lever so she cannot remove her head.
2. With the warm, sterilized wipe or cloth, clean the udder and teats to remove any dirt, manure, or bacteria that may be present. Then, place the metal bucket on the stand below the udder.
3. Wrap your thumb and forefinger around the base of one teat. This will help trap the milk in the teat so it can be squirted out. Then, starting with your middle finger, squeeze the three remaining fingers in one single, smooth motion to squirt the milk into the bucket. Be sure to keep a tight grip on the base of the teat so the milk stays there until extracted. The first squirt of milk from either teat should not be put into the bucket, as it may contain dirt or bacteria that you don't want contaminating the milk.

4. Release the grip on the teat and allow it to refill with milk. While this is happening, you can repeat this process on the other teat and alternate between teats to speed up the milking process.
5. When the teats begin to look empty (they will be somewhat flat in appearance), massage the udder just a little bit to see if any more milk remains. If so, squeeze it out in the same manner as above until you cannot extract much more.
6. Remove the milk bucket from the stand and then, with your teat-dip mixture in a disposable cup, dip each teat into the solution and allow to air-dry. This will keep bacteria and infection from going into the teat and udder.
7. Remove the goat from the milk stand and return her to the pen.

Making Cheese from Goat Milk

Most varieties of cheese that can be made from cow's milk can also be successfully made using goat milk. Goat milk cheese can easily be made at home. To make the cheese, however, at least 1 gallon of goat milk should be available. Make sure that all of your equipment is washed and sterilized (using heat is fine) before using it.

Cottage Cheese
1. Collect surplus milk that is free of strong odors. Cool it to around 40°F and keep it at that temperature until it is used.
2. Skim off any cream. Use the skim milk for cheese and the cream for cheese dressing.
3. If you wish to pasteurize your milk (which will allow it to hold better as a cheese) collect all the milk to be processed into a flat-bottomed, straight-sided pan and heat to 145°F on low heat. Hold it at this temperature for about 30 minutes and then cool to around 80°F. Use a dairy thermometer to measure the milk's temperature. Then, inoculate the cheese milk with a desirable lactic acid–fermenting bacterial culture (you can use commercial buttermilk for the initial source). Add about 7 ounces to 1 gallon of cheese milk, stir well, and let it sit undisturbed for about 10 to 16 hours, until a firm curd is formed.
4. When the curd is firm enough, cut the curd into uniform cubes no larger than ½ inch using a knife or spatula.

5. Allow the curd to sit undisturbed for a couple of minutes and then warm it slowly, stirring carefully, at a temperature no greater than 135°F. The curd should eventually become firm and free from whey.

6. When the curd is firm, remove from the heat and stop stirring. Siphon off the excess whey from the top of the pot. The curd should settle to the bottom of the container. If the curd is floating, bacteria that produces gas has been released and a new batch must be made.

7. Replace the whey with cold water, washing the curd and then draining the water. Wash again with ice-cold water to chill the curd. This will keep the flavor fresh.

8. Using a draining board, drain the excess water from the curd. Now your curd is complete.

9. To make the curd into a cottage cheese consistency, separate the curd as much as possible and mix with a milk or cream mixture containing salt to taste.

Domiati Cheese

This type of cheese is made throughout the Mediterranean region. It is eaten fresh or aged 2 to 3 months before consumption.

1. Cool a gallon of fresh, quality milk to around 105°F, adding 8 ounces of salt to the milk. Stir the salt until it is completely dissolved.

2. Pasteurize the milk as described in step 3 of the cottage cheese recipe.

3. This type of cheese is coagulated by adding a protease enzyme (rennet). This enzyme may be purchased at a local drug store, a health food store, or a cheesemaker in your area.

Dissolve the concentrate in water, add it to the cheese milk, and stir for a few minutes. Use 1 milliliter of diluted rennet liquid in 40 milliliters of water for every 2½ gallons of cheese milk.

4. Set the milk at around 105°F. When the enzyme is completely dispersed in the cheese milk, allow the mix to sit undisturbed until it forms a firm curd.

5. When the desired firmness is reached, cut the curd into very small cubes. Allow for some whey separation. After 10 to 20 minutes, remove and reserve about one-third the volume of salted whey.

6. Put the curd and remaining whey into cloth-lined molds (the best are rectangular stainless steel containers with perforated sides and bottoms) with a cover. The molds should be between 7 and 10 inches in height. Fill the molds with the curd, fold the cloth over the top, allow the whey to drain, and discard the whey.

7. Once the curd is firm enough, apply added weight for 10 to 18 hours until it is as moist as you want.

8. Once the pressing is complete and the cheese is formed into a block, remove the molds and cut the blocks into 4-inch-thick pieces. Place the pieces in plastic containers with airtight seals. Fill the containers with reserved salted whey from step 5, covering the cheese by about an inch.

9. Place these containers at a temperature between 60°F and 65°F to cure for 1 to 4 months.

Feta Cheese

For feta cheese, the same process is used as the Domiati cheese except that salt is not added to the milk before coagulation. Feta cheese is aged in a brine solution after the cubes have been salted in a brine solution for at least 24 hours.

Keeping Dairy Cows

Raising dairy cows is difficult work. It takes time, energy, resources, and dedication. There are many monthly expenses for feeds, medicines, vaccinations, and labor. However, when managed properly, a small dairy farmer can reap huge benefits, like extra cash and the pleasure of having fresh milk available daily.

Breeds

There are thousands of different breeds of cows, but what follows are the three most popular breeds of dairy cows.

The Holstein cow has roots tracing back almost 2,000 years ago to European migrant tribes. Today, the breed is widely popular in the United States for its exceptional milk production. These cows are large animals, typically marked with spots of jet black and pure white.

The Ayrshire breed takes its name from the county of Ayr in Scotland. Throughout the early nineteenth century, Scottish breeders carefully crossbred strains of cattle to develop a cow well suited to the climate of Ayr and with a large, flat udder best suited for the production of Scottish butter and cheese. The uneven terrain and the erratic climate of their native land explain their ability to adapt to all types of surroundings and conditions. Ayrshire cows are not only strong and resilient, but their trim, well-rounded outline and red and predominantly white color have made them easily recognized as one of the most beautiful of the dairy cattle breeds.

The Jersey breed is one of the oldest breeds, originating from Jersey of the Channel Islands. Jersey cows are known for their ring of fine hair around the nostrils and their milk rich in butterfat. Averaging a total body weight of around 900 pounds, the Jersey cow produces the most pounds of milk per pound of body weight when compared to all other breeds.

Housing

There are many factors to consider when choosing housing for your cattle, including budget, preference, breed, and circumstance. Free-stall barns provide a clean, dry, comfortable resting area and easy access to food and water. If designed properly, the cows are not restrained and are free to enter, lie down, rise, and leave the barn whenever they desire. They are usually built with concrete walkways and raised stalls with steel dividing bars. The floor of the stalls may be covered with various materials, ideally a sanitary inorganic material such as sand.

A flat barn is another popular alternative, which requires tie-chains or stanchions to keep the cows in their stalls. However, it creates a need for cows to be routinely released into an open area for exercise. It is also very important that the stalls are designed to fit the physical characteristics of the cows. For example, the characteristically shorter Jersey cows should not be housed in a stall designed for much larger Holsteins.

A compost-bedded pack barn, generally known as a compost dairy barn, allows cows to move freely, promising increased cow comfort. Though it requires exhaustive pack and ventilation management, it can notably reduce manure storage costs.

Grooming

Cows with sore feet and legs can often lead to losses from milk production, diminished breeding efficiency, and lameness. Hoof trimming is essential to help prevent these outcomes, though it is often very labor intensive, allowing it to be easily neglected. Hoof trimming should be supervised or taught by a veterinarian until you get the hang of it. A simple electric clipper will keep your cows well groomed and clean. Mechanical cow brushes are another option. These brushes can be installed in a free-stall dairy barn, allowing cows to groom themselves using a rotating brush that activates when rubbed against.

Feeding and Watering

In the summer months, cows can receive most of their nutrition from grazing, assuming there is plenty of pasture. You may need to rotate areas of pasture so that the grass has an opportunity to grow back before the cows are let loose in that area again. Grazing pastures should include higher-protein grasses, such as alfalfa, clover, or lespedeza. During the winter, cows should be fed hay. Plan to offer the cows 2 to 3 pounds of high-quality hay per 100 pounds of body weight per day. This should provide adequate nutrition for the cows to produce 10 quarts of milk per day, during peak production months. To increase production, supplement feed with ground corn, oats, barley, and wheat bran. Proper mixes are available from feed stores.

See page 117 for recipes for homemade cheese, yogurt, and ice cream.

Allowing cows access to a salt block will also help to increase milk production. Water availability and quantity is crucial to health and productivity. Water intake varies; however, it is important that cows are given the opportunity to consume a large amount of clean water several times a day. Generally, cows consume 30 to 50 percent of their daily water intake within an hour of milking. Water quality can also be an issue. Some of the most common water quality problems affecting livestock are high concentrations of minerals and bacterial contamination. Send out 1 to 2 quarts of water from the source to be tested by a laboratory recommended by your veterinarian.

To run an organic dairy, cows must receive feed that was grown without the use of pesticides, commercial fertilizers, or genetically modified ingredients, along with other restrictions.

Common Diseases Affecting Cows

Pinkeye and foot rot are two of the most prevalent conditions affecting all breeds of cattle of all ages year-round. Though both diseases are non-fatal, they should be taken seriously and treated by a qualified veterinarian.

Wooden tongue occurs worldwide, generally appearing in areas where there is a copper deficiency or the cattle graze on land with rough grass or weeds. It affects the tongue, causing it to become hard and swollen so that eating is painful for the animal. Surgical intervention is often required.

Brucellosis, or Bang's, is the most common cause of abortion in cattle. The milk produced by an infected cow can also contain the bacteria, posing a threat to the health of humans.

Keeping Pigs

Pigs can be farm-raised on a commercial scale for profit, in smaller herds to provide fresh, homegrown meat for your family, or to be shown and judged at county fairs or livestock shows. Characterized by their stout bodies, short legs, snouts, hooves, and thick, bristle-coated skin, pigs are omnivorous, garbage-disposing mammals that, on a small farm, can be difficult to turn a profit on but yield great opportunities for fair showmanship and quality food on your dinner table.

Breeds

Pigs of different breeds have different functionalities—some are known for their terminal sire (the ability to produce offspring intended for slaughter rather than for further breeding) and have a greater potential to pass along desirable traits, such as durability, leanness, and quality of meat, while others are known for their reproductive and maternal qualities. The breed you choose to raise will depend on whether you are raising your pigs for show, for profit, or for putting food on your family's table.

Eight Major US Pig Breeds

Yorkshire—Originally from England, this large white breed of hog has a long frame, comparable to the Landrace. They are known for their quality meat and mothering ability and are likely the most widely distributed breed of pig in the world. Farmers will also find that the Yorkshire breed generally adapts well to confinement.

Landrace—This white-haired hog is a descendent from Denmark and is known for producing large litters, supplying milk, and exhibiting good maternal qualities. The breed is long-bodied and short-legged with a nearly flat arch to its back. Its long, floppy ears are droopy and can cover its eyes.

Chester—Like the Landrace, this popular white hog is known for its mothering abilities and large litter size. Originating from crossbreeding in Pennsylvania, Chester hogs are medium-sized and solid white in color.

Berkshire—Originally from England, the black-and-white Berkshire hog has perky ears and a short, dished snout. This medium-sized breed is known for its siring ability and quality meat.

Duroc—Ranging from solid colors of light gold to dark red, the strongly built Durocs are known for their rapid growth and ultra-efficient feed-to-meat conversion. This large breed is also hailed for its tasty meat.

Poland China—Known for often reaching the maximum weight at any age bracket, this black-and-white breed is of the meaty variety.

Hampshire—A likely descendent of an old English breed, the Hampshire is one of America's oldest original breeds. Characterized by a white belt circling the front of the pigs' black bodies, this breed is known for its hardiness and high-quality meat.

Spot—Known for producing pigs with high growth rates, this black-and-white spotted hog gains weight quickly while maintaining a favorable feed efficiency. Part of the Spot's ancestry can be traced back to the Poland China breed.

Housing Pigs

Keeping your pigs happy and healthy and preventing them from wandering off requires two primary structures: a shelter and a sturdy fence. A shelter is necessary to protect your pigs from inclement weather and to provide them with plenty of shade, as their skin is prone to sunburn. Shelters can be relatively simple three-sided, roofed structures with slanted, concrete flooring to allow you to spray away waste with ease. To help keep your pigs comfortable, provide them with enough straw in their shelter and an area to make a wallow—a muddy hole they can lie in to stay cool.

Because pigs will use their snouts to dig and pry their way through barriers, keeping these escape artists fenced in can pose a challenge. "Hog wire," or woven fence wire, at least 40 inches high is commonly used for perimeter fencing. You can line the top and especially the bottom of your fence with a strand of barbed or electric wire to discourage your pigs from tunneling their way through. If you use electric wiring, you may have a difficult time driving your herd through the gate. Covering the gate with non-electric panels using woven wire, metal, or wood can make coaxing your pigs from the pasture an easier task.

Feeding Your Pigs

Pigs are of the omnivorous variety, and there isn't much they won't eat. Swine will consume anything from table and garden scraps to insects and worms, to grass, flowers, and trees. Although your pigs won't turn their snouts up to garbage, a cost-effective approach to ensuring good health and a steady growth rate for your pigs is to supply farm grains (mixed at home or purchased commercially), such as oats, wheat, barley, soybeans, and corn. Cornmeal and soybean meal are a good source of energy that fits well into a pig's low-fiber, high-protein diet requirements. Use non-GMO varieties of corn and soybean to raise organic pork. For best results, you should include protein supplements and vitamins in farm grain diets.

As pigs grow, their dietary needs change, which is why feeding stages are often classified as starter, grower, and finisher. Your newly weaned piglets make up the starting group, pigs 50 to 125 pounds are growing, and those between the 125- and 270-pound market weight are finishing pigs.

As your pigs grow, they will consume more feed and should transition to a less dense, reduced-protein diet. You should let your pigs self-feed during every stage. In other words, allow them to consume the maximum amount they will take in a single feeding. Letting your pigs self-feed once or twice a day allows them to grow and gain weight quickly.

Another essential part of feeding is to make sure you provide a constant supply of fresh, clean water. Your options range from automatic watering systems to water barrels. Your pigs can actually go longer without feed than they can without water, so it's important to keep them hydrated.

Common Diseases Affecting Pigs

Just like with humans, pigs can build up their immune systems by maintaining a healthy lifestyle, including a balanced diet and plenty of exercise. Being sure your pigs have space to roam, a clean living environment, and nutrient-rich food will go a long way in keeping your livestock healthy. You can help to prevent the most common pig diseases from affecting your herd by asking your veterinarian about vaccination programs. Common diseases include *E. coli*—a bacteria typically caused by contaminated fecal matter in the living environment that causes piglets to experience diarrhea. Many people advise to vaccinate female pigs for *E. coli* before they begin farrowing. Another common pig disease is erysipelas, which is caused by bacteria that pigs secrete through their saliva or waste products. Heart infections and chronic arthritis are possible ailments the bacteria cause in pigs that can lead to death. Some farmers inoculate pregnant females and newly bought feeder pigs to defend against this prevalent disease.

Other diseases to watch out for are atrophic rhinitis, characterized by inflammation of a pig's nasal tissues; leptospirosis, an easily spreadable bacteria-borne disease; and porcine parvovirus, an intestinal virus that can spread without showing symptoms.

Q & A

Q: Should I vaccinate my organic pigs?

A: In the United States, vaccinating pigs against common diseases is allowed—and even encouraged—when raising pigs for certified organic pork. However, many diseases can be prevented by providing your pigs with quality feed, a clean environment, enough natural light, and opportunities to exercise. When pigs do become ill, they should be separated from the other livestock to prevent disease from spreading.

Food from Scratch

Canning

Canning is fun, economical, and a good way to preserve your precious produce. As more and more farmers' markets make their way into urban centers, city dwellers are also discovering how rewarding it is to make seasonal treats last all year round. Besides the value of your labor, canning homegrown or locally grown food may save you half the cost of buying commercially canned food. Freezing food may be simpler, but most people have limited freezer space, whereas cans of food can be stored almost anywhere. And what makes a nicer, more thoughtful gift than a jar of homemade jam, tailored to match the recipient's favorite fruits and flavors?

The nutritional value of home canning is an added benefit. Many vegetables begin to lose their vitamins as soon as they are harvested. Nearly half the vitamins may be lost within a few days unless the fresh produce is kept cool or preserved. Within 1 to 2 weeks, even refrigerated produce loses half or more of certain vitamins. The heating process during canning destroys from one-third to one-half of vitamins A and C, thiamin, and riboflavin. Once canned, foods may lose from 5 to 20 percent of these sensitive vitamins each year. The amounts of other vitamins, however, are only slightly lower in canned compared to fresh food. If vegetables are handled properly and canned promptly after harvest, they can be more nutritious than fresh produce sold in local stores.

The advantages of home canning are lost when you start with poor-quality foods, when jars fail to seal properly, when food spoils, and when flavors, texture, color, and nutrients deteriorate during prolonged storage. The tips that follow explain many of these problems and recommend ways to minimize them.

How Canning Preserves Foods

The high percentage of water in most fresh foods makes them very perishable. They spoil or lose their quality for several reasons:

- Growth of undesirable microorganisms—bacteria, molds, and yeasts
- Activity of food enzymes
- Reactions with oxygen
- Moisture loss

Microorganisms live and multiply quickly on the surfaces of fresh food and on the inside of bruised, insect-damaged, and diseased food. Oxygen and enzymes are present throughout fresh food tissues. Proper canning practices include:

- Carefully selecting and washing fresh foods
- Peeling some fresh foods
- Hot packing many foods
- Adding acids (lemon juice, citric acid, or vinegar) to some foods
- Using acceptable jars and self-sealing lids
- Processing jars in a boiling-water or pressure canner for the correct amount of time

Collectively, these practices remove oxygen; destroy enzymes; prevent the growth of undesirable bacteria, yeasts, and molds; and help form a high vacuum in jars. High vacuums form tight seals, which keep liquid in and air and microorganisms out.

TIP

A large stockpot with a lid can be used in place of a boiling-water canner for high-acid foods like tomatoes, pickles, apples, peaches, and jams. Simply place a rack inside the pot so that the jars do not rest directly on the bottom of the pot.

Food Acidity and Processing Methods

Whether food should be processed in a pressure canner or boiling-water canner to control botulism bacteria depends on the acidity in the food. Acidity may be natural, as in most fruits, or added, as in pickled food.

Low-acid canned foods contain too little acidity to prevent the growth of these bacteria. Other foods may contain enough acidity to block their growth or to destroy them rapidly when heated. The term "pH" is a measure of acidity: the lower its value, the more acidic the food. The acidity level in foods can be increased by adding lemon juice, citric acid, or vinegar.

Low-acid foods have pH values higher than 4.6. They include red meats, seafood, poultry, milk, and all fresh vegetables except for most tomatoes. Most products that are mixtures of low-acid and acid foods also have pH values above 4.6 unless their ingredients include enough lemon juice, citric acid, or vinegar to make them acid foods. Acid foods have a pH of 4.6 or lower. They include fruits, pickles, sauerkraut, jams, jellies, marmalade, and fruit butters.

Although tomatoes usually are considered an acid food, some are now known to have pH values slightly above 4.6. Figs also have pH values slightly above 4.6. Therefore, if they are to be canned as acid foods, these products must be acidified to a pH of 4.6 or lower with lemon juice or citric acid. Properly acidified tomatoes and figs are acid foods and can be safely processed in a boiling-water canner.

Botulinum spores are very hard to destroy at boiling-water temperatures; the higher the canner temperature, the more easily they are destroyed. Therefore, all low-acid foods should be sterilized at temperatures of 240 to 250°F, attainable with pressure canners operated at 10 to 15 PSIG. (PSIG means pounds per square inch of pressure as measured by a gauge.)

At these temperatures, the time needed to destroy bacteria in low-acid canned foods ranges from 20 to 100 minutes. The exact time depends on the kind of food being canned, the way it is packed into jars, and the size of jars. The time needed to safely process low-acid foods in boiling water ranges from 7 to 11 hours; the time needed to process acid foods in boiling water varies from 5 to 85 minutes.

Know Your Altitude

It is important to know your approximate elevation or altitude above sea level in order to determine a safe processing time for canned foods. Since the boiling temperature of liquid is lower at higher elevations, it is critical that additional time be given for the safe processing of foods at altitudes above sea level.

What Not to Do

Open-kettle canning and the processing of freshly filled jars in conventional ovens, microwave ovens, and dishwashers are not recommended because these practices do not prevent all risks of spoilage. Steam canners are not recommended because processing times for use with current models have not been adequately researched. Because steam canners may not heat foods in the same manner as boiling-water canners, their use with boiling-water processing times may result in spoilage. So-called canning powders are useless as preservatives and do not replace the need for proper heat processing.

It is not recommended that pressures in excess of 15 PSIG be applied when using new pressure-canning equipment.

Ensuring High-Quality Canned Foods

Examine food carefully for freshness and wholesomeness. Discard diseased and moldy food. Trim small diseased lesions or spots from food.

Can fruits and vegetables picked from your garden or purchased from nearby producers when the products are at their peak of quality—within 6 to 12 hours after harvest for most vegetables. However, apricots, nectarines, peaches, pears, and plums should be ripened 1 or more days between harvest and canning. If you must delay the canning of other fresh produce, keep it in a shady, cool place.

Fresh, home-slaughtered red meats and poultry should be chilled and canned without delay. Do not can meat from sickly or diseased animals. Put fish and seafood on ice after harvest, eviscerate immediately, and can them within 2 days.

Maintaining Color and Flavor in Canned Food

To maintain good natural color and flavor in stored canned food, you must:

- Remove oxygen from food tissues and jars.
- Quickly destroy the food enzymes.
- Obtain high jar vacuums and airtight jar seals.

Follow these guidelines to ensure that your canned foods retain optimal colors and flavors during processing and storage:

- Use only high-quality foods that are at the proper maturity and are free of diseases and bruises.
- Use the hot-pack method, especially with acid foods to be processed in boiling water.
- Don't unnecessarily expose prepared foods to air; can them as soon as possible.
- While preparing a canner-load of jars, keep peeled, halved, quartered, sliced, or diced apples, apricots, nectarines, peaches, and pears in a solution of 3 grams (3,000 milligrams) ascorbic acid to 1 gallon of cold water. This procedure is also useful in maintaining the natural color of mushrooms and potatoes and for preventing stem-end discoloration in cherries and grapes.

You can get ascorbic acid in several forms:

Pure powdered form—Seasonally available among canning supplies in supermarkets. One level teaspoon of pure powder weighs about 3 grams. Use 1 teaspoon per gallon of water as a treatment solution.

Vitamin C tablets—Economical and available year-round in many stores. Buy 500-milligram tablets; crush and dissolve 6 tablets per gallon of water as a treatment solution.

Commercially prepared mixes of ascorbic and citric acid—Seasonally available among canning supplies in supermarkets. Sometimes citric acid powder is sold in supermarkets, but it is less effective at controlling discoloration. If you choose to use these products, follow the manufacturer's directions.

- Fill hot foods into jars and adjust headspace as specified in recipes.
- Tighten screw bands securely, but if you are especially strong, not as tightly as possible.
- Process and cool jars.

- Store the jars in a relatively cool, dark place, preferably between 50 and 70°F.
- Can no more food than you will use within a year.

Advantages of Hot Packing

Many fresh foods contain from 10 percent to more than 30 percent air. The length of time that food will last at premium quality depends on how much air is removed from the food before jars are sealed. The more air that is removed, the higher the quality of the canned product.

Raw packing is the practice of filling jars tightly with freshly prepared but unheated food. Such foods, especially fruit, will float in the jars. The entrapped air in and around the food may cause discoloration within 2 to 3 months of storage. Raw packing is more suitable for vegetables processed in a pressure canner.

Hot packing is the practice of heating freshly prepared food to boiling, simmering it 3 to 5 minutes, and promptly filling jars loosely with the boiled food. Hot packing is the best way to remove air and is the preferred pack style for foods processed in a boiling-water canner. At first, the color of hot-packed foods may appear no better than that of raw-packed foods, but within a short storage period both the color and flavor of hot-packed foods will be superior.

Whether food has been hot packed or raw packed, the juice, syrup, or water to be added to the foods should be heated to boiling before it is added to the jars. This practice helps to remove air from food tissues, shrinks food, helps keep the food from floating in the jars, increases vacuum in sealed jars, and improves shelf life. Preshrinking food allows you to add more food to each jar.

Controlling Headspace

The unfilled space above the food in a jar and below its lid is termed headspace. It is best to leave a ¼-inch headspace for jams and jellies, ½ inch for fruits and tomatoes to be processed in boiling water, and from 1 to 1¼ inches for low-acid foods to be processed in a pressure canner.

This space is needed for expansion of food as jars are processed and for forming vacuums in cooled jars. The extent of expansion is determined by the air content in the food and by the processing temperature. Air expands greatly when heated to high temperatures—the higher the temperature, the greater the expansion. Foods expand less than air when heated.

Jars and Lids

Food may be canned in glass jars or metal containers. Metal containers can be used only once. They require special sealing equipment and are much more costly than jars.

Mason-type jars designed for home canning are ideal for preserving food by pressure or boiling-water canning. Regular- and wide-mouthed threaded mason jars with self-sealing lids are the best choices. They are available in half-pint, pint, 1½-pint, and quart sizes. The standard jar mouth opening is about 2⅜ inches. Wide-mouthed jars have openings of about 3 inches, making them more easily filled and emptied. Regular-mouthed decorative jelly jars are available in 8-ounce and 12-ounce sizes.

With careful use and handling, mason jars may be reused many times, requiring only new lids each time. When lids are used properly, jar seals and vacuums are excellent.

Jar Cleaning

Before reuse, wash empty jars in hot water with detergent and rinse well by hand, or wash in a dishwasher. Rinse thoroughly, as detergent residue may cause unnatural flavors and colors. Scale or hard-water films on jars are easily removed by soaking jars several hours in a solution containing 1 cup of vinegar (5 percent acid) per gallon of water.

Sterilization of Empty Jars

Use sterile jars for all jams, jellies, and pickled products processed less than 10 minutes. To sterilize empty jars, put them right side up on the rack in a boiling-water canner. Fill the canner and jars with hot (not boiling) water to 1 inch above the tops of the jars. Boil 10 minutes. Remove and drain hot sterilized jars one at a time. Save the hot water for processing filled jars. Fill jars with food, add lids, and tighten screw bands.

Empty jars used for vegetables, meats, and fruits to be processed in a pressure canner need not be sterilized beforehand. It is also unnecessary to sterilize jars for fruits, tomatoes, and pickled or fermented foods that will be processed 10 minutes or longer in a boiling-water canner.

Lid Selection, Preparation, and Use

The common self-sealing lid consists of a flat metal lid held in place by a metal screw band during processing. The flat lid is crimped around its bottom edge to form a trough, which is filled with a colored gasket material. When jars are processed, the lid gasket softens and flows slightly to cover the jar-sealing surface, yet allows air to escape from the jar. The gasket then forms an airtight seal as the jar cools. Gaskets in unused lids work well for at least 5 years from the date of manufacture. The gasket material in older unused lids may fail to seal on jars.

It is best to buy only the quantity of lids you will use in a year. To ensure a good seal, carefully follow the manufacturer's directions in preparing lids for use. Examine all metal lids carefully. Do not use old, dented, or deformed lids or lids with gaps or other defects in the sealing gasket.

After filling jars with food, release air bubbles by inserting a flat plastic (not metal) spatula between the food and the jar. Slowly turn the jar and move the spatula up and down to allow air bubbles to escape. Adjust the headspace and then clean the jar rim (sealing surface) with a dampened paper towel. Place the lid, gasket down, onto the cleaned jar-sealing surface. Uncleaned jar-sealing surfaces may cause seal failures.

Then fit the metal screw band over the flat lid. Follow the manufacturer's guidelines on or enclosed with the box for tightening the jar lids properly.

- If screw bands are too tight, air cannot vent during processing, and food will discolor during storage. Overtightening also may cause lids to buckle and jars to break, especially with raw-packed, pressure-processed food.
- If screw bands are too loose, liquid may escape from jars during processing, seals may fail, and the food will need to be reprocessed.

Do not retighten lids after processing jars. As jars cool, the contents in the jar contract, pulling the self-sealing lid firmly against the jar to form a high vacuum. Screw bands are not needed on stored jars. They can be removed easily after jars are cooled. When removed, washed, dried, and stored in a dry area, screw bands may be used many times. If left on stored jars, they become difficult to remove, often rust, and may not work properly again.

Selecting the Correct Processing Time

When food is canned in boiling water, more processing time is needed for most raw-packed foods and for quart jars than is needed for hot-packed foods and pint jars.

To destroy microorganisms in acid foods processed in a boiling-water canner, you must:

- Process jars for the correct number of minutes in boiling water.
- Cool the jars at room temperature.

To destroy microorganisms in low-acid foods processed with a pressure canner, you must:

- Process the jars for the correct number of minutes at 240°F (10 PSIG) or 250°F (15 PSIG).
- Allow canner to cool at room temperature until it is completely depressurized.

The food may spoil if you fail to use the proper processing times, fail to vent steam from canners properly, process at lower pressure than specified, process for fewer minutes than specified, or cool the canner with water.

Processing times for half-pint and pint jars are the same, as are times for 1½-pint and quart jars. For some products, you have a choice of processing at 5, 10, or 15 PSIG. In these cases, choose the canner pressure (PSIG) you wish to use and match it with your pack style (raw or hot) and jar size to find the correct processing time.

Recommended Canners

There are two main types of canners for heat processing home-canned food: boiling-water canners and pressure canners. Most are designed to hold seven 1-quart jars or eight to nine 1-pint jars. Small pressure canners hold four 1-quart jars; some large pressure canners hold eighteen 1-pint jars in two layers but hold only seven 1-quart jars. Pressure saucepans with smaller volume capacities are not recommended for use in canning. Treat small pressure canners the same as standard larger canners; they should be vented using the typical venting procedures.

Low-acid foods must be processed in a pressure canner to be free of botulism risks. Although pressure canners also may be used for processing acid foods, boiling-water canners are recommended because they are faster. A pressure canner would require from 55 to 100 minutes to can a load of jars; the total time for canning most acid foods in boiling water varies from 25 to 60 minutes.

A boiling-water canner loaded with filled jars requires about 20 to 30 minutes of heating before its water begins to boil. A loaded pressure canner requires about 12 to 15 minutes of heating before it begins to vent, another 10 minutes to vent the canner, another 5 minutes to pressurize the canner, another 8 to 10 minutes to process the acid food, and, finally, another 20 to 60 minutes to cool the canner before removing jars.

Boiling-Water Canners

These canners are made of aluminum or porcelain-covered steel. They have removable perforated racks and fitted lids. The canner must be deep enough so that at least 1 inch of briskly boiling water will cover the tops of jars during processing. Some boiling-water canners do not have flat bottoms. A flat bottom must be used on an electric range. Either a flat or ridged bottom can be used on a gas burner. To ensure uniform processing of all jars with an electric range, the canner should be no more than 4 inches wider in diameter than the element on which it is heated.

Using a Boiling-Water Canner

Follow these steps for successful boiling-water canning:

1. Fill the canner halfway with water.
2. Preheat water to 140°F for raw-packed foods and to 180°F for hot-packed foods.
3. Load filled jars, fitted with lids, into the canner rack and use the handles to lower the rack into the water; or fill the canner, one jar at a time, with a jar lifter.
4. Add more boiling water, if needed, so the water level is at least 1 inch above jar tops.
5. Turn heat to its highest position until water boils vigorously.
6. Set a timer for the minutes required for processing the food.
7. Cover with the canner lid and lower the heat setting to maintain a gentle boil throughout the processing time.
8. Add more boiling water, if needed, to keep the water level above the jars.
9. When jars have been boiled for the recommended time, turn off the heat and remove the canner lid.
10. Using a jar lifter, remove the jars and place them on a towel, leaving at least 1 inch of space between the jars during cooling.

Pressure Canners

Pressure canners for use in the home have been extensively redesigned in recent years. Models made before the 1970s were heavy-walled kettles with clamp-on lids. They were fitted with a dial gauge, a vent port in the form of a petcock or counterweight, and a safety fuse. Modern pressure canners are lightweight, thin-walled kettles; most have turn-on lids. They have a jar rack, a gasket, a dial or weighted gauge, an automatic vent or cover lock, a vent port (steam vent) that is closed with a counterweight or weighted gauge, and a safety fuse.

Pressure does not destroy microorganisms, but high temperatures applied for a certain period of time do. The success of destroying all microorganisms capable of growing in canned food is based on the temperature obtained in pure steam, free of air, at sea level. At sea level, a canner operated at a gauge pressure of 10 pounds provides an internal temperature of 240°F.

Air trapped in a canner lowers the inside temperature and results in under-processing. The highest volume of air trapped in a canner occurs when processing raw-packed foods in dial-gauge canners. These canners do not vent air during processing. To be safe, all types of pressure canners must be vented 10 minutes before they are pressurized.

To vent a canner, leave the vent port uncovered on newer models or manually open petcocks on some older models. Heating the filled canner with its lid locked into place boils water and generates steam that escapes through the petcock or vent port. When steam first escapes, set a timer for 10 minutes. After venting 10 minutes, close the petcock or place the counterweight or weighted gauge over the vent port to pressurize the canner.

Weighted-gauge models exhaust tiny amounts of air and steam each time their gauge rocks or jiggles during processing. The sound of the weight rocking or jiggling indicates that the canner is maintaining the recommended pressure and needs no further attention until the load has been processed for the set time. Weighted-gauge canners cannot correct precisely for higher altitudes, and at altitudes above 1,000 feet must be operated at a pressure of 15.

Check dial gauges for accuracy before use each year and replace if they read high by more than 1 pound at 5, 10, or 15 pounds of pressure. Low readings cause over-processing and may indicate that the accuracy of the gauge is unpredictable. If a gauge is consistently low, you may adjust the processing pressure. For example, if the directions call for 12 pounds of pressure and your dial gauge has tested 1 pound low, you can safely process at 11 pounds of pressure. If the gauge is more than 2 pounds low, it is unpredictable, and it is best to replace it. Gauges may be checked at most USDA county extension offices, which are located in every state across the country.

Handle gaskets of canner lids carefully and clean them according to the manufacturer's directions. Nicked or dried gaskets will allow steam leaks during pressurization of canners. Gaskets of older canners may need to be lightly coated with vegetable oil once per year, but newer models are pre-lubricated. Check your canner's instructions.

Lid safety fuses are thin metal inserts or rubber plugs designed to relieve excessive pressure from the canner. Do not pick at or scratch fuses while cleaning lids. Use only canners that have Underwriter's Laboratory (UL) approval to ensure their safety.

Replacement gauges and other parts for canners are often available at stores offering canner equipment or from canner manufacturers. To order parts, list the canner model number and describe the parts needed.

Using a Pressure Canner

Follow these steps for successful pressure canning:

1. Put 2 to 3 inches of hot water in the canner. Place filled jars on the rack, using a jar lifter. Fasten canner lid securely.
2. Open petcock or leave weight off vent port. Heat at the highest setting until steam flows from the petcock or vent port.
3. Maintain high heat setting, exhaust steam 10 minutes, and then place weight on vent port or close petcock. The canner will pressurize during the next 3 to 5 minutes.
4. Start timing the process when the pressure reading on the dial gauge indicates that the recommended pressure has been reached or when the weighted gauge begins to jiggle or rock.
5. Regulate heat under the canner to maintain a steady pressure at or slightly above the correct gauge pressure. Quick and large pressure variations during processing may cause unnecessary liquid losses from jars. Weighted gauges on Mirro canners should jiggle about two or three times per minute. On Presto canners, they should rock slowly throughout the process.

When processing time is completed, turn off the heat, remove the canner from heat if possible, and let the canner depressurize. Do not force-cool the canner. If you cool it with cold running water in a sink or open the vent port before the canner depressurizes by itself, liquid will spurt from jars, causing low liquid levels and jar seal failures. Force-cooling also may warp the canner lid of older model canners, causing steam leaks.

Depressurization of older models should be timed. Standard-size heavy-walled canners require about 30 minutes when loaded with pints and

45 minutes with quarts. Newer thin-walled canners cool more rapidly and are equipped with vent locks. These canners are depressurized when their vent lock piston drops to a normal position.

1. After the vent port or petcock has been open for 2 minutes, unfasten the lid and carefully remove it. Lift the lid away from you so that the steam does not burn your face.

2. Remove jars with a lifter, and place on towel or cooling rack, if desired.

Cooling Jars

Cool the jars at room temperature for 12 to 24 hours. Jars may be cooled on racks or towels to minimize heat damage to counters. The food level and liquid volume of raw-packed jars will be noticeably lower after cooling because air is exhausted during processing and food shrinks. If a jar loses excessive liquid during processing, do not open it to add more liquid. As long as the seal is good, the product is still usable.

Testing Jar Seals

After cooling jars for 12 to 24 hours, remove the screw bands and test seals with one of the following methods:

Method 1: Press the middle of the lid with a finger or thumb. If the lid springs up when you release your finger, the lid is unsealed and reprocessing will be necessary.

Method 2: Tap the lid with the bottom of a teaspoon. If it makes a dull sound, the lid is not sealed. If food is in contact with the underside of the lid, it will also cause a dull sound. If the jar lid is sealed correctly, it will make a ringing, high-pitched sound.

Method 3: Hold the jar at eye level and look across the lid. The lid should be concave (curved down slightly at the center). If the center of the lid is either flat or bulging, it may not be sealed.

Reprocessing Unsealed Jars

If a jar fails to seal, remove the lid and check the jar-sealing surface for tiny nicks. If necessary, change the jar, add a new, properly prepared lid, and reprocess within 24 hours using the same processing time.

Another option is to adjust headspace in unsealed jars to 1½ inches and freeze jars and contents instead of reprocessing. However, make sure jars have straight sides. Freezing may crack jars with "shoulders."

Foods in single unsealed jars could be stored in the refrigerator and consumed within several days.

Storing Canned Foods

If lids are tightly vacuum-sealed on cooled jars, remove screw bands, wash the lid and jar to remove food residue, then rinse and dry jars. Label and date the jars and store them in a clean, cool, dark, dry place. Do not store jars at temperatures above 95°F or near hot pipes, a range, a furnace; in an un-insulated attic; or in direct sunlight. Under these conditions, food will lose quality in a few weeks or months and may spoil. Dampness may corrode metal lids, break seals, and allow recontamination and spoilage.

Accidental freezing of canned foods will not cause spoilage unless jars become unsealed and recontaminated. However, freezing and thawing may soften food. If jars must be stored where they may freeze, wrap them in newspapers, place them in heavy cartons, and cover them with more newspapers and blankets.

Identifying and Handling Spoiled Canned Food

Growth of spoilage bacteria and yeast produces gas, which pressurizes the food, swells lids, and breaks jar seals. As each stored jar is selected for use, examine its lid for tightness and vacuum. Lids with concave centers have good seals.

Next, while holding the jar upright at eye level, rotate the jar and examine its outside surface for streaks of dried food originating at the top of the jar. Look at the contents for rising air bubbles and unnatural color.

While opening the jar, smell for unnatural odors and look for spurting liquid and cotton-like mold growth (white, blue, black, or green) on the top food surface and underside of lid. Do not taste food from a stored jar you discover to have an unsealed lid or that otherwise shows signs of spoilage.

All suspect containers of spoiled low-acid foods should be treated as having produced botulinum toxin and should be handled carefully as follows:

- If the suspect glass jars are unsealed, open, or leaking, they should be detoxified before disposal.
- If the suspect glass jars are sealed, remove lids and detoxify the entire jar, contents, and lids.

Detoxification Process

Carefully place the suspect containers and lids on their sides in an 8-quart-volume or larger stockpot, pan, or boiling-water canner. Wash your hands thoroughly. Carefully add water to the pot. The water should completely cover the containers with a minimum of 1 inch of water above the containers. Avoid splashing the water. Place a lid on the pot and heat the water to boiling. Boil 30 minutes to ensure detoxifying the food and all container components. Cool and discard lids and food in the trash or bury in the soil.

Thoroughly clean all counters, containers, and equipment including can opener, clothing, and hands that may have come in contact with the food or the containers. Discard any sponges or washcloths that were used in the cleanup. Place them in a plastic bag and discard in the trash.

Pectin is a substance that helps foods gel and it occurs naturally in many fruits. Some fruits have enough pectin that you don't need to add much (if any) to make jelly out of them. How do you know which fruits contain pectin? Do the bounce test! Fruits that tend to bounce when you drop them a short distance (like blueberries, blackberries, and lemons) have more pectin than those that just squish when dropped (like strawberries or peaches).

Apple Butter

The best apple varieties to use for apple butter include Jonathan, Winesap, Stayman, Golden Delicious, and Macintosh apples, but any of your favorite varieties will work. Don't bother to peel the apples, as you will strain the fruit before cooking it anyway. This recipe will yield 8 to 9 pints.

Ingredients
- 8 pounds apples
- 2 cups cider
- 2 cups vinegar
- 2¼ cups white sugar
- 2¼ cups packed brown sugar
- 2 tablespoons ground cinnamon
- 1 tablespoons ground cloves

Directions
1. Wash, stem, quarter, and core apples.
2. Cook slowly in cider and vinegar until soft. Press fruit through a colander, food mill, or strainer.
3. Cook fruit pulp with sugar and spices, stirring frequently. To test for doneness, remove a spoonful and hold it away from steam for 2 minutes. If the butter remains mounded on the spoon, it is done. If you're still not sure, spoon a small quantity onto a plate. When a rim of liquid does not separate around the edge of the butter, it is ready for canning.
4. Fill hot into sterile half-pint or pint jars, leaving ¼-inch headspace. Quart jars need not be pre-sterilized.

PROCESS TIMES FOR APPLE BUTTER IN A BOILING-WATER CANNER*

Style of Pack	Jar Size	Process Time at Altitudes of		
		0–1,000 ft	1,001–6,000 ft	Above 6,000 ft
Hot	Half-pints or Pints	5 minutes	10 minutes	15 minutes
	Quarts	10 minutes	15 minutes	20 minutes

*After the process is complete, turn off the heat and remove the canner lid. Wait 5 minutes before removing jars.

Strawberry-Rhubarb Jelly

Strawberry-rhubarb jelly will turn any ordinary piece of bread into a delightful treat. You can also spread it on shortcake or pound cake for a simple and unique dessert. This recipe yields about seven half-pints.

Ingredients
- 1½ pounds red stalks of rhubarb
- 1½ quarts ripe strawberries
- ½ teaspoon butter or margarine to reduce foaming (optional)
- 6 cups sugar
- 6 ounces liquid pectin

Directions
1. Wash and cut rhubarb into 1-inch pieces and blend or grind. Wash, stem, and crush strawberries, one layer at a time, in a saucepan. Place both fruits in a jelly bag or double layer of cheesecloth and gently squeeze juice into a large measuring cup or bowl.
2. Measure 3½ cups of juice into a large saucepan. Add butter and sugar, thoroughly mixing into juice. Bring to a boil over high heat, stirring constantly.
3. As soon as mixture begins to boil, stir in pectin. Bring to a full rolling boil and boil hard 1 minute, stirring constantly. Remove from heat, quickly skim off foam, and fill sterile jars, leaving ¼-inch headspace. Adjust lids and process.

PROCESS TIMES FOR STRAWBERRY-RHUBARB JELLY IN A BOILING-WATER CANNER*

Style of Pack	Jar Size	Process Time at Altitudes of		
		0–1,000 ft	1,001–6,000 ft	Above 6,000 ft
Hot	Half-pints or Pints	5 minutes	10 minutes	15 minutes
*After the process is complete, turn off the heat and remove the canner lid. Wait 5 minutes before removing jars.				

Crushed Tomatoes

Crushed tomatoes are great for use in soups, stews, thick sauces, and casseroles. Simmer crushed tomatoes with kidney beans, chili powder, sautéed onions, and garlic to make an easy pot of chili.

Directions

1. Wash tomatoes and dip in boiling water for 30 to 60 seconds or until skins split. Then dip in cold water, slip off skins, and remove cores. Trim off any bruised or discolored portions and quarter.
2. Heat ⅙ of the quarters quickly in a large pot, crushing them with a wooden mallet or spoon as they are added to the pot. This will exude juice. Continue heating the tomatoes, stirring to prevent burning.
3. Once the tomatoes are boiling, gradually add remaining quartered tomatoes, stirring constantly. These remaining tomatoes do not need to be crushed; they will soften with heating and stirring. Continue until all tomatoes are added. Then boil gently 5 minutes.
4. Add bottled lemon juice or citric acid to jars (see page 93). Add 1 teaspoon of salt per quart to the jars, if desired. Fill jars immediately with hot tomatoes, leaving ½-inch headspace. Adjust lids and process.

PROCESS TIMES FOR CRUSHED TOMATOES IN
A DIAL-GAUGE PRESSURE CANNER*

Style of Pack	Jar Size	Process Time	Canner Gauge Pressure (PSI) at Altitudes of			
			0–2,000 ft	2,001–4,000 ft	4,001–6,000 ft	6,001–8,000 ft
Hot	Pints or Quarts	20 minutes	6 lb	7 lb	8 lb	9 lb
		15 minutes	11 lb	12 lb	13 lb	14 lb

*After the canner is completely depressurized, remove the weight from the vent port or open the petcock. Wait 10 minutes, then unfasten the lid and remove it carefully. Lift the lid with the underside away from you so that the steam coming out of the canner does not burn your face.

PROCESS TIMES FOR CRUSHED TOMATOES IN A WEIGHTED-GAUGE PRESSURE CANNER*

Style of Pack	Jar Size	Process Time	Canner Gauge Pressure (PSI) at Altitudes of	
			0–1,000 ft	Above 1,000 ft
Hot	Pints or Quarts	20 minutes	5 lb	10 lb
		15 minutes	10 lb	15 lb

*After the canner is completely depressurized, remove the weight from the vent port or open the petcock. Wait 10 minutes, then unfasten the lid and remove it carefully. Lift the lid with the underside away from you so that the steam coming out of the canner does not burn your face.

Homemade Butter, Cheese, and Ice Cream

Make Your Own Butter

Making butter the old-fashioned way is incredibly simple and very gratifying. It's a great project to do with kids, too. All you need is a jar, a marble, some fresh cream, and about 20 minutes.

Directions

1. Start with about twice as much heavy whipping cream as you'll want butter. Pour it into the jar, drop in the marble, close the lid tightly, and start shaking.
2. Check the consistency of the cream every 3 to 4 minutes. The liquid will turn into whipped cream, and then eventually you'll see little clumps of butter forming in the jar. Keep shaking for another few minutes and then begin to strain out the liquid into another jar. This is buttermilk, which is great for use in making pancakes, waffles, biscuits, and muffins.

3. The butter is now ready, but it will store better if you wash and work it. Add ½ cup of ice-cold water and continue to shake for 2 or 3 minutes. Strain out the water and repeat. When the strained water is clear, mash the butter to extract the last of the water, and strain.
4. Scoop the butter into a bowl, a ramekin, a mold, or wax paper.

If desired, add salt or chopped fresh herbs to your butter just before storing or serving. Butter can also be made in a food processor or blender to speed up the processing time.

Make Your Own Yogurt

Yogurt is basically fermented milk. You can make it by adding the active cultures *Streptococcus thermophilus* and *Lactobacillus bulgaricus* to heated milk, which will produce lactic acid, creating yogurt's tart flavor and thick consistency. Yogurt is simple to make and is delicious on its own, as a dessert, in baked goods, or in place of sour cream.

Yogurt is thought to have originated many centuries ago among the nomadic tribes of Eastern Europe and Western Asia. Milk stored in animal skins would acidify and coagulate. The acid helped preserve the milk from further spoilage and from the growth of pathogens (disease-causing microorganisms).

Ingredients
Makes 4 to 5 cups of yogurt

- 1 quart milk (cream, whole, low-fat, or skim)—In general, the higher the milk fat level in the yogurt, the creamier and smoother it will taste. Note: If you use home-produced milk it *must* be pasteurized before preparing yogurt.
- Nonfat dry milk powder—Use ⅓ cup powder when using whole or low-fat milk, or use ⅔ cup powder when using skim milk. The higher the milk solids, the firmer the yogurt will be. For even more firmness, add gelatin (directions below).
- Commercial, unflavored, cultured yogurt—Use ¼ cup. Be sure the product label indicates that it contains a live culture. Also note the content of the culture. *L. bulgaricus* and *S. thermophilus* are required

in yogurt, but some manufacturers may in addition add *L. acidophilus* or *B. bifidum*. The latter two are used for slight variations in flavor, but more commonly for health reasons attributed to these organisms. All culture variations will make a successful yogurt.
- 2 to 4 tablespoons sugar or honey (optional)
- 1 teaspoon unflavored gelatin (optional)—For a thick, firm yogurt, swell 1 teaspoon gelatin in a little milk for 5 minutes. Add this to the milk and nonfat dry milk mixture before cooking.

Supplies
- Double boiler or regular saucepan—1 to 2 quarts in capacity larger than the volume of yogurt you wish to make.
- Cooking or jelly thermometer—A thermometer that can clip to the side of the saucepan and remain in the milk works best. Accurate temperatures are critical for successful processing.
- Mixing spoon.
- Yogurt containers—Cups with lids or canning jars with lids.
- Incubator—A yogurt-maker, oven, heating pad, or warm spot in your kitchen. To use your oven, place yogurt containers into deep pans of 110°F water. Water should come at least halfway up the containers. Set oven temperature at lowest point to maintain water temperature at 110°F. Monitor temperature throughout incubation, making adjustments as necessary.

Processing
1. Combine ingredients and heat. Heating the milk is necessary in order to change the milk proteins so that they set together rather than form curds and whey. Do not substitute this heating step for pasteurization. Place cold, pasteurized milk into top of a double boiler and stir in nonfat dry milk powder. Adding nonfat dry milk to heated milk will cause some milk proteins to coagulate and form strings. Add sugar or honey if a sweeter, less tart yogurt is desired. Heat milk to 200°F, stirring gently, and hold for 10 minutes for thinner yogurt or hold 20 minutes for thicker yogurt. Do not boil. Be careful and stir constantly to avoid scorching if not using a double boiler.
2. Cool and inoculate. Place the top of the double boiler in cold water to cool milk rapidly to 112 to 115°F. Remove 1 cup of the warm milk and

blend it with the yogurt starter culture. Add this to the rest of the warm milk. The temperature of the mixture should now be 110 to 112°F.

3. Incubate. Pour immediately into clean, warm containers; cover and place in prepared incubator. Close the incubator and incubate about 4 to 7 hours at 110°F, ± 5°F. Yogurt should set firmly when the proper acid level is achieved (pH 4.6). Incubating yogurt for several hours after the yogurt has already set will produce more acidity. This will result in a more tart or acidic flavor and eventually cause the whey to separate.

4. Refrigerate. Rapid cooling stops the development of acid. Yogurt will keep for about 10 to 21 days if held in the refrigerator at 40°F or lower.

Yogurt Types

Set yogurt: A solid set where the yogurt firms in a container and is not disturbed.

Stirred yogurt: Yogurt made in a large container, then spooned or otherwise dispensed into secondary serving containers. The consistency of the "set" is broken and the texture is less firm than that of set yogurt. This is the most popular form of commercial yogurt.

Drinking yogurt: Stirred yogurt into which additional milk and flavors are mixed. Add fruit or fruit syrups to taste. Mix in milk to achieve the desired thickness. The shelf life of this product is 4 to 10 days, since the pH is raised by the addition of fresh milk. Some whey separation will occur and is natural. Commercial products recommend a thorough shaking before consumption.

Fruit yogurt: Fruit, fruit syrups, or pie filling can be added to the yogurt. Place them on top, at the bottom, or stir them into the yogurt.

Troubleshooting

- If milk forms some clumps or strings during the heating step, some milk proteins may have gelled. Take the solids out with a slotted spoon or, in difficult cases, after cooking pour the milk mixture through a clean colander or cheesecloth before inoculation.
- When yogurt fails to coagulate (set) properly, it's because the pH is not low enough. Milk proteins will coagulate when the pH has dropped to 4.6. This is done by the culture growing and producing

acids. Adding culture to very hot milk (+115°F) can kill bacteria. Use a thermometer to carefully control temperature.

- If yogurt takes too long to make, it may be because the temperature is off. Too hot or too cold of an incubation temperature can slow down culture growth. Use a thermometer to carefully control temperature.
- If yogurt just isn't working, it may be because the starter culture was of poor quality. Use a fresh, recently purchased culture from the grocery store each time you make yogurt.
- If yogurt tastes or smells bad, it's likely because the starter culture was contaminated. Obtain new culture for the next batch.
- If yogurt has over-set or incubated too long, make sure to refrigerate yogurt immediately after a firm coagulum has formed.
- If yogurt tastes a little odd, it could be due to over-heating or boiling of the milk. Use a thermometer to carefully control temperature.
- When whey collects on the surface of the yogurt, it's called syneresis. Some syneresis is natural. Excessive separation of whey, however, can be caused by incubating yogurt too long or by agitating the yogurt while it is setting.

Storing Your Yogurt

- Always pasteurize milk or use commercially pasteurized milk to make yogurt.
- Discard batches that fail to set properly, especially those due to culture errors.
- Yogurt generally has a 10- to 21-day shelf life when made and stored properly in the refrigerator below 40°F.
- Always use clean and sanitized equipment and containers to ensure a long shelf life for your yogurt. Clean equipment and containers in hot water with detergent, then rinse well. Allow to air-dry.

Yogurt in an Instant Pot

If you own an Instant Pot, by all means, use that yogurt button and follow the directions. The Instant Pot will boil the milk, then you let it cool and whisk in the starter, and then you let it incubate—all right in the same pot!

Make Your Own Cheese

There are endless varieties of cheese you can make, but they all fall into two main categories: soft and hard. Soft cheeses (like cream cheese) are easier to make because they don't require a cheese press. The curds in hard cheeses (like cheddar) are pressed together to form a solid block or wheel, which requires more time and effort, but hard cheeses will keep longer than soft cheeses, and generally have a much stronger flavor.

Cheese is basically curdled milk and is made by adding an enzyme (typically rennet) to milk, allowing curds to form, heating the mixture, straining out the whey, and finally pressing the curds together. Cheeses such as *queso fresco* or *queso blanco* (traditionally eaten in Latin American countries) and *paneer* (traditionally eaten in India) are made with an acid such as vinegar or lemon juice instead of bacterial cultures or rennet.

You can use any kind of milk to make cheese, including cow's milk, goat's milk, sheep's milk, and even buffalo's milk (used for traditional mozzarella). For the richest flavor, try to get raw milk from a local farmer. If you don't know of one near you, visit www.realmilk.com/where.html for a listing of raw milk suppliers in your state. You can use homogenized milk, but it will produce weaker curds and a milder flavor. If your milk is pasteurized, you'll need to "ripen" it by heating it in a double boiler until it reaches 86°F and then adding 1 cup of unpasteurized, preservative-free cultured buttermilk per gallon of milk and letting it stand 30 minutes to 3 hours (the longer you leave it, the sharper the flavor will be). If you cannot find unpasteurized buttermilk, diluting ⅛ teaspoon calcium chloride (available from online cheesemaker suppliers) in ¼ cup of water and adding it to your milk will create a similar effect.

For a goat cheese recipe, see page 76.

Rennet (also called rennin or chymosin) is sold online at cheesemaking sites in tablet or liquid form. You may also be able to find Junket rennet tablets near the pudding and gelatin at your grocery store. One teaspoon of liquid rennet is the equivalent of 1 rennet tablet, which is enough to turn 5 gallons of milk into cheese (estimate 4 drops of liquid rennet per gallon of milk). Microbial rennet is a vegetarian alternative that is available for purchase online.

Preparation

It's important to keep your hands clean and all equipment sterile when making cheese.

1. Wash hands and all equipment with soapy detergent before and after use.
2. Rinse all equipment with clean water, removing all soapy residue.
3. Boil all cheesemaking equipment between uses.
4. For best-quality cheese, use new cheesecloth each time you make cheese. (Sterilize cheesecloth by first washing, then boiling.)
5. Squeaky clean is clean. If you can feel a residue on the equipment, it is not clean.

Yogurt Cheese

This soft cheese has a flavor similar to sour cream and a texture like cream cheese. A pint of yogurt will yield approximately ¼ pound of cheese. The yogurt cheese has a shelf life of approximately 7 to 14 days when wrapped and placed in the refrigerator and kept at less than 40°F. Add a little salt and pepper and chopped fresh herbs for variety.

Directions

1. Line a large strainer or colander with cheesecloth.
2. Place the lined strainer over a bowl and pour in plain, whole-milk yogurt. Do not use yogurt made with the addition of gelatin, as gelatin will inhibit whey separation.
3. Let yogurt drain overnight, covered with plastic wrap. Empty the whey from the bowl.
4. Fill a strong plastic storage bag with some water, seal, and place over the cheese to weigh it down. Let the cheese stand another 8 hours and then enjoy!

Queso Blanco

Queso blanco is a white, semi-hard cheese made without culture or rennet. It is often eaten fresh and may be flavored with peppers, herbs, and spices. It is also considered a "frying cheese," meaning it does not melt and may be deep-fried or grilled. Queso blanco is best eaten fresh, so try this small recipe the first time you make it. If it disappears quickly, next time double or triple the recipe. This recipe will yield about ½ cup of cheese.

Ingredients
- 2 cups milk
- 4 teaspoons white vinegar
- Salt
- Minced jalapeño, black pepper, chives, or other herbs to taste

Directions
1. Heat milk to 176°F for 20 minutes.
2. Add vinegar slowly to the hot milk until the whey is semi-clear and the curd particles begin to form stretchy clumps. Stir for 5 to 10 minutes. When it's ready you should be able to stretch a piece of curd about ⅓ inch before it breaks.
3. Allow to cool, and strain off the whey by filtering through a cheesecloth-lined colander or a cloth bag.
4. Work in salt and spices to taste.
5. Press the curd in a mold or simply leave in a ball.
6. *Queso blanco* may keep for several weeks if stored in a refrigerator, but is best eaten fresh.

Ricotta Cheese

Making ricotta is very similar to making queso blanco, though it takes a bit longer. Start the cheese in the morning for use at dinner, or make a day ahead. Use it in lasagna, in desserts, or all on its own.

Ingredients
- 1 gallon milk
- ¼ teaspoon salt
- ⅓ cup plus 1 teaspoon white vinegar

Directions
1. Pour milk into a large pot, add salt, and heat slowly while stirring until the milk reaches 180°F.
2. Remove from heat and add vinegar. Stir for 1 minute as curds begin to form.
3. Cover and allow to sit undisturbed for 2 hours.
4. Pour mixture into a colander lined with cheesecloth, and allow to drain for 2 or more hours.
5. Store in a sealed container for up to a week.

Mozzarella

This mild cheese will make your homemade pizza especially delicious. Or slice it and eat with fresh tomatoes and basil from the garden. Fresh cheese can be stored in salt water but must be eaten within 2 days.

Ingredients
- 1 gallon 2% milk
- ¼ cup fresh, plain yogurt (see recipe on page 118)
- 1 tablet rennet or 1 teaspoon liquid rennet dissolved in ½ cup tap water
- Brine: Use 2 pounds of salt per gallon of water

Directions
1. Heat milk to 90°F and add yogurt. Stir slowly for 15 minutes while keeping the temperature constant.
2. Add rennet mixture and stir for 3 to 5 minutes.
3. Cover, remove from heat, and allow to stand until coagulated, about 30 minutes.
4. Cut curd into ½-inch cubes. Allow to stand for 15 minutes with occasional stirring.
5. Return to heat and slowly increase temperature to 118°F over a period of 45 minutes. Hold this temperature for an additional 15 minutes.
6. Drain off the whey by transferring the mixture to a cheesecloth-lined colander. Use a spoon to press the liquid out of the curds. Transfer the mat of curd to a flat pan that can be kept warm in a low oven. Do not cut mat, but turn it over every 15 minutes for a 2-hour period. Mat should be tight when finished.
7. Cut the mat into long strips 1 to 2 inches wide and place in hot water (180°F). Using wooden spoons, tumble and stretch it under water until it becomes elastic, about 15 minutes.
8. Remove curd from hot water and shape it by hand into a ball or a loaf, kneading in the salt. Place cheese in cold water (40°F) for approximately 1 hour.
9. Store in a solution of 2 teaspoons salt to 1 cup water.

Cheddar Cheese

Cheddar is a New England and Wisconsin favorite. The longer you age it, the sharper the flavor will be. Try a wedge with a slice of homemade apple pie.

Ingredients
- 1 gallon milk
- ¼ cup buttermilk
- 1 tablet rennet or 1 teaspoon liquid rennet
- 1½ teaspoons salt

Directions
1. Combine milk and buttermilk and allow the mixture to ripen overnight.
2. The next day, heat milk to 90°F in a double boiler and add rennet.
3. After about 45 minutes, cut curds into small cubes and let sit 15 minutes.
4. Heat very slowly to 100°F and cook for about an hour or until a cooled piece of curd will keep its shape when squeezed.
5. Drain curds and rinse out the double boiler.
6. Place a rack lined with cheesecloth inside the double boiler and spread the curds on the cloth. Cover and reheat at about 98°F for 30 to 40 minutes. The curds will become one solid mass.
7. Remove the curds, cut them into 1-inch-wide strips, and return them to the pan. Turn the strips every 15 to 20 minutes for 1 hour.
8. Cut the strips into cubes and mix in salt.
9. Let the curds stand for 10 minutes, place them in cheesecloth, and press in a cheese press with 15 pounds for 10 minutes, then with 30 pounds for an hour.

(Continued on next page)

10. Remove the cheese from the press, unwrap it, dip in warm water, and fill in any cracks.
11. Wrap again in cheesecloth and press with 40 pounds for 24 hours.
12. Remove from the press and let the cheese dry about 5 days in a cool, well-ventilated area, turning the cheese twice a day and wiping it with a clean cloth. When a hard skin has formed, rub with oil or seal with wax. You can eat the cheese after 6 weeks, but for the strongest flavor, allow cheese to age for 6 months or more.

Homemade Ice Cream

Supplies
- 1-pound coffee can
- 3-pound coffee can
- Duct tape
- Ice
- 1 cup salt (rock salt is best, but table salt will also work)

Ingredients
- 2 cups half-and-half
- ½ cup sugar
- 1 teaspoon vanilla

Directions
1. Mix all the ingredients in the 1-pound coffee can. Cover the lid with duct tape to ensure it is tightly sealed.
2. Place the smaller can inside the larger can and fill the space between the two with ice and salt.
3. Cover the large can and seal with duct tape. Roll the can back and forth for 15 minutes. To reduce noise, place a towel on your working surface, or work on a rug.
4. Dump out ice and water. Stir contents of small can. Store ice cream in a glass or plastic container (if you leave it in the can it may take on a metallic flavor).

If desired, add cocoa powder, coffee granules, crushed peppermint sticks or other candy, or fruit.

Fermenting

Fermenting is the process of preserving certain food products using either bacteria or yeast and keeping exposure to air to a minimum. Fermentation is used to help preserve certain foods and to create new flavors. This process is used to create products such as kefir, sauerkraut, and kombucha, which are full of healthy probiotics that aid digestion and strengthen the immune system.

TIP

When fermenting anything, make sure all your utensils are clean. Wash all containers and utensils with hot soapy water prior to use. Otherwise, you run the risk of introducing bad bacteria into your food, ruining the whole batch.

Kefir

Kefir is slightly fermented milk. It is similar to yogurt, except it is milder in flavor and of a thinner consistency.

To make kefir you will need to obtain kefir "grains," which are made up of yeast and bacteria. These can be purchased online, or at select health food stores. The grains will vary in size—anywhere from rice to walnut size—and they resemble pieces of cauliflower.

Rinse the grains. Add about ½ cup grains to 1 quart of milk. The milk should be cold, preferably directly from the fridge. The milk can be store-bought, and skim or low-fat milk works best. Cover the milk, but do not seal it tightly, and leave it to sit at room temperature for 24 to 48 hours. Stir the milk once a day. Test the milk occasionally after the 24-hour period—finished kefir should have a mildly acidic taste and be slightly carbonated. Strain the grains from the kefir and refrigerate it. Rinse the grains.

The grains will continue to grow and multiply as they are used. Occasionally, some grains will have to be removed from the milk mixture to ensure it does not become too thick. Remove the extra grains, wash them in cold water, and allow them to dry completely between two pieces of cheesecloth.

To revive either dried or new grains place them in 1 cup of milk for 24 hours. Drain out the grains, rinse them, and add them back to the milk, with another cup of fresh milk added. After 2 days you can add enough milk to make 1 quart and create kefir using the normal process.

Kefir grains.

Lacto-fermented Sauerkraut

Sauerkraut is the simple process of fermenting cabbage. The only things necessary are salt, cabbage, and a non-metal crock to put the cabbage in.

Mix shredded cabbage and salt in a large pot and let it sit for 15 minutes. If desired, add a few shredded carrots as well. For 1 medium head of cabbage you'll need about 1½ tablespoons kosher salt. As the cabbage sits, the salt will draw moisture out of the cabbage leaves and begin to pool in the pot. Massaging the cabbage or crushing it with a potato masher will help speed up the process. Pack the cabbage and liquid into a clean crock or wide-mouthed mason jar. Use a wooden spoon to press the cabbage tightly into the crock. Make sure that the juices from the cabbage and salt mixture cover the cabbage. If they do not, some water may be added. Cover the cabbage with cheesecloth, tucking it down the edges of the crock. Use a heavy lid or a smaller jar to weigh down the cabbage. Cover the jar with cheesecloth and place on a counter or in a cupboard away from direct sunlight. Ferment the cabbage for 3 to 10 days, tasting it after 3 days to see if it's zingy enough for you. If scum builds up on the surface while the sauerkraut is fermenting, remove it with a clean spoon. When the flavor is right, cover the jar with a tight-fitting lid and refrigerate. It will keep in the refrigerator for at least 2 months.

TIP

You might think the "lacto" part of lacto-fermenting has something to do with dairy products, but actually it refers to *Lactobacillus*, a beneficial bacteria on the surface of fruits and vegetables. During the fermenting process, the *Lactobacillus* converts sugars into lactic acid, which serves as a preservative.

Lacto-fermented Vegetables

Cabbage is not the only veggie that can be fermented. Carrots, peppers, beets, and (of course) cucumbers are all great candidates for lacto-fermentation. For 3 cups of chopped or sliced veggies, you'll need to combine 1 quart of water with 3 tablespoons sea salt, kosher salt, or pickling salt. Place the vegetables in a clean glass jar with a tight-fitting lid. Pour the salt-water brine over the vegetables, being sure they're fully submerged and that there's 1 inch of headspace at the top of the jar. If desired, add a tablespoon of minced garlic, a bay leaf, a pinch of peppercorns, red pepper flakes, other dried herbs, and/or a couple of grape leaves (which will help keep the veggies crisp).

Screw the lid onto the jar and let sit at room temperature, away from direct sunlight, for several days. Every day or two, unscrew the lid slightly to allow pressure to escape. Skim off any scum that forms along the surface. After a few days taste the veggies to see if they're "ripe" enough for your taste. If so, move jar to the refrigerator. If not, continue to let ferment until they're ready.

Kombucha

Kombucha is a medicinal tea full of healthy probiotics that aid digestion and the immune system. It is brewed by fermenting tea using a mass of yeast and bacteria that forms the kombucha culture, called the SCOBY (symbiotic "colony" of bacteria and yeast). It's gelatinous, rather creepy-looking, and jam-packed with healthiness. Every batch of kombucha will create a new layer on the SCOBY, which can be peeled off and shared or discarded. So the best way to get started is to ask someone who is already brewing kombucha if you can have a layer of their SCOBY and a couple cups of kombucha to use as a starter. Alternately, you can purchase SCOBYs online. Don't skip the sugar in this recipe—it's essential to the fermenting process. However, the bacteria eat the sugar, so the end result is a tea that is fizzy and just barely sweet.

Simple Kombucha

Ingredients
- 1½ quarts water
- ½ cup granulated sugar
- 4 bags green or black tea
- 1 SCOBY
- 1 cup already brewed kombucha

Directions
1. Bring the water to a boil, remove from heat, stir in the sugar, and add the tea bags. Allow the tea to brew until water is lukewarm and then remove the tea bags.
2. Add the brewed kombucha and pour into a clean 2-quart glass jar. Place the SCOBY into the jar with the tea, cover with cheesecloth or a paper towel, and secure with a rubber band.
3. Leave the jar at room temperature in a cupboard or somewhere where there's little direct light. Try not to disturb the jar while it's brewing. In about a week you should start to see bubbles floating around the SCOBY. Pour a little of the tea into a glass and taste it. If it's fizzy, it's ready to drink. Pour into a new jar and refrigerate, leaving a couple of inches of kombucha in the jar with the SCOBY to keep it healthy until you brew another batch. If you'd like it fizzier, let it ferment a few more days.

TIP

Check your SCOBY for any signs of mold. Any green spots mean that it has been compromised. Discard both the kombucha and SCOBY, and begin again.

Grinding and Sprouting Grains

The part of the wheat, buckwheat, barley, or other grains that we consume is the seed. Flour is the grain seeds ground into a fine powder. White flour has had the germ of the seed removed before being ground up, and since most of the fiber, vitamins B and E, and minerals are in the germ, white flour doesn't provide much nutrition. When you grind grains into flour yourself, you ensure that you're getting all the nutritional benefits of the whole grain. Fresh flour also contains more nutrients than flour that's been exposed to the air for a while. There are oils in flour that go rancid quickly, and as that happens, many of the nutrients are diminished.

A good grain mill will pay for itself before long, since un-ground whole organic grains are much cheaper than buying organic flours. You can purchase hand-operated grain mills or electric ones—or even hybrid mills—online, and they range in price from about $25 to over $1,000. Most are adjustable so that you can choose a really fine or a coarser grind. Hand-crank mills require a little more time and effort, but they won't increase your electric bill and you'll get a little arm workout in. Some mills can also be used to make nut butters or to grind coffee beans, but not all are that versatile. The more expensive mills tend to have stronger motors, have more versatility in the coarseness of the grain and in what you can grind (both dry and wet ingredients), have more attractive designs, and come with lengthy warranties. You can also grind grain in a Vitamix with a dry container or in other high-quality blenders. KitchenAid stand mixers have a grain mill attachment you can use for low-oil grains.

Purchase wheat berries (the whole grains) or whatever whole grain you choose in the bulk section of natural food stores or online. Grind only what you'll be using right away. If you find you have a little extra, store it in the freezer for up to a few days. Any longer and the oils may start to go rancid and you'll lose many of the nutrients.

Soaking grains helps to break down some of the components of grains that many people find difficult to digest, and also releases many valuable nutrients. Phytic acid is an antinutrient, which is something that works against the body's ability to absorb certain vitamins or minerals. Phytic acid, which is found in many grains, inhibits absorption of zinc, iron, phosphorous and magnesium. Phytase is an enzyme that is also found in most grains and helps to break down the phytic acid. Soaking grains with something acidic activates this process. Although our stomachs are pretty good at soaking things in acid, these days many of our digestive systems are compromised to some degree and can use a little extra help.

You can soak whole grains or flour. Put the grain in a bowl, add enough warm water to cover the grain, and splash some vinegar, lemon juice, buttermilk, kefir, or yogurt into the bowl. If you're the kind of person who likes to measure things, it's 1 tablespoon of an acidic medium for every 1 cup of warm water. Stir, cover tightly, and let sit at room temperature. The length of time you should soak varies according to the grain. After soaking, you can dry the grains in a dehydrator or in your oven at a low temperature, or you can use them wet, adjusting your recipe to accommodate the extra liquid.

Grain	Soak Time for Soaked Grains	Soak Time before Sprouting	Sprout Time
Barley	12–24 hours	6–8 hours	2 days
Brown rice	7 hours	9 hours	3–5 days
Buckwheat	7 hours	15 minutes	1–2 days
Corn	12–24 hours	12 hours	2–3 days
Kamut	12–24 hours	7 hours	2–3 days
Millet	7 hours	8 hours	2–3 days
Oats	12–24 hours	6 hours	2–3 days
Quinoa	12–24 hours	2 hours	1–2 days
Rye	12–24 hours	8 hours	2–3 days
Spelt	12–24 hours	8 hours	2–3 days

TIP

To use soaked flour in a bread recipe, combine all the liquid in the recipe with the flour, except replace 2 tablespoons of the water with apple cider vinegar, lemon juice, or another acid, cover, and allow to soak before proceeding with the rest of the recipe.

To make cookies with soaked flour, combine the flour with all the wet ingredients and soak in the refrigerator for 4 hours or overnight. Then add remaining ingredients, mix, and bake.

Sprouting grains is the process of germinating the grain seeds, which decreases the starch in the grain and increases the protein, fat, and vitamin B. You can sprout whole grains in large batches, dry them, and then grind them when you're ready to bake. Only whole grains can be sprouted—not flour or even hulled grains.

To sprout wheat berries or other whole grains, rinse and drain them in a colander. Transfer to a bowl, cover with a couple inches of water, and allow to soak at room temperature overnight. Then drain and rinse them again. Dump the grains into a mason jar and cover it with cheesecloth secured with a rubber band. Once a day, pour water into the jar, swirl it around, and drain it out. Leave the jar at an angle out of direct sunlight and facing downward into a dish or the sink so it can continue to drain. Within 1 to 5 days you should see the grains begin to sprout. You can let the sprouts continue to grow up to ¼ inch. Then rinse, drain, and refrigerate the sprouted grains, or dry them in a dehydrator or in the oven at a low temperature. Once the grains are dry, you can grind them into flour.

Natural Cleaners and Bath Products

Bath Salts and Cosmetics

Lavender Bath Salt

Pour several tablespoons of this into your bath as it fills for an extra-soothing, relaxing, and cleansing experience. You can also add powdered milk or finely ground old-fashioned oatmeal to make your skin especially soft. Toss in a few lavender buds if you have them.

Ingredients
2 cups coarse sea salt
½ cup Epsom salts
½ cup baking soda
4 to 6 drops lavender essential oil
2 tablespoons dried flower petals or lavender buds

Directions
Mix all ingredients thoroughly and store in a glass jar or other airtight container.

Citrus Scrub

Use this invigorating scrub to wake up your senses in the morning. The vitamin C in oranges serves as an astringent, making it especially good for oily skin.

Ingredients
½ lemon, orange, or grapefruit
3 tablespoons cornmeal
2 tablespoons Epsom salts or coarse sea salt

Directions
Squeeze citrus juice and pulp into a bowl and add cornmeal and salts. Add more juice to make a paste or less for bath salts. Rub gently over entire body and then rinse.

Healing Bath Soak

This bath soak will relax tired muscles, help to calm nerves, and leave skin soft and fragrant. You may also wish to add blackberry, raspberry, or violet leaves. Dried or fresh herbs can be used.

Ingredients
2 tablespoons comfrey leaves
1 tablespoon lavender
1 tablespoon evening primrose flowers
1 teaspoon orange peel, thinly sliced or grated
2 tablespoons oatmeal

Directions
Combine herbs and tie up in a small muslin or cheesecloth sack. Leave under faucet as the tub fills with hot water. If desired, empty herbs into the bathwater once the tub is full.

See page 35 for tips on growing herbs in pots.

Honey Lip Gloss

Homemade lip gloss containers can be any small glass jar or tin, or you can reuse an old lip gloss container (just make sure all the old gloss is out of the container). To sterilize the container, wash with soap and hot water, dunk the container in a jar of rubbing alcohol, rinse clean, and then allow the container to completely dry before pouring in your melted gloss.

Ingredients
1 teaspoon beeswax (you can find this at a craft store or at your local farmers' market)
½ teaspoon honey
2 teaspoons almond oil (optional)
Vitamin E oil from a capsule (optional)

Directions
1. Melt the beeswax and honey in a heat-proof jar in the microwave or use a double boiler method.
2. When the wax and honey are just melted, remove from the heat source and whisk in the almond oil and vitamin E oil, if you so desire. To remove the vitamin E oil from the capsule, simply prick the end of the capsule with a safety pin and squeeze it out.
3. Pour the mixture into the containers and allow to cool fully before using.

Note: If you want to add a citrus flavoring to this lip gloss, you can add a few drops of lemon or lime essential oil during the whisking stage.

After-Sun Comfrey Lotion

Comfrey root soothes skin and minimizes inflammation. Apply this lotion to sunburned skin for immediate relief and faster healing.

Ingredients
3 tablespoons fresh comfrey root
1 cup water
1 tablespoon beeswax, unrefined
¾ cup sweet almond oil or light cooking oil
¼ cup cocoa butter
4 vitamin E capsules
¼ cup aloe vera gel
1 teaspoon borax powder
12 to 16 drops essential oil (peppermint, lavender, and sandalwood are all good choices)

Directions
1. Place the comfrey root and water in a small pot and bring to a boil, simmering for about 30 minutes. Strain, retaining the water. Discard the root.
2. In a double boiler, combine beeswax, oil, and cocoa butter, stirring over low heat until melted. Remove from heat. Pierce the vitamin E capsules and add the oil from inside, stirring to combine.
3. In a separate saucepan, combine the comfrey water, aloe vera gel, and borax powder, stirring over low heat until the borax is fully dissolved. Allow to cool.
4. Once both mixtures are cooled to room temperature, pour the beeswax and oil mixture in a thin stream into the comfrey water mixture, whisking vigorously to combine (or use a food processor). Add the essential oil and continue mixing until thoroughly combined.
5. Cover and store in a cool, dark place.

Shampoo, Conditioner, and Body Cleansers

Shampoo

Cleaning your hair can be as simple as making a baking soda and water paste, scrubbing it into your hair, and rinsing well. However, if you enjoy the feel of a sudsy, soapy, scented shampoo, try this recipe. You can substitute homemade soap flakes for the castile soap, if desired.

Ingredients
4 ounces liquid castile soap
3 tablespoons fresh or dried herbs of your choice, boiled for 30 minutes in 2 cups water and strained

Directions
Pour the soap and herbal water into a jar, cover, and shake until well combined.

Hair Conditioner

This conditioner will add softness and volume to your hair. Avocados, bananas, and egg yolks are also great hair conditioners. Apply conditioner, allow to sit in hair a minimum of 5 minutes (longer for a deeper conditioning), and then rinse well. You may wish to shampoo a second time after using this conditioner.

Ingredients
1 cup olive oil
1 teaspoon lemon juice
1 teaspoon cider vinegar
2 teaspoons honey
6 to 10 drops essential oil, if desired

Directions
Whisk all ingredients together or blend in a food processor. Store in an airtight container.

Herbs for Your Hair

Herbs for dry hair	Burdock root, comfrey, elderflowers, lavender, marshmallow, parsley, sage, stinging nettle
Herbs for oily hair	Calendula, horsetail, lemon juice, lemon balm, mint, rosemary, witch hazel, yarrow
Herbs to combat dandruff	Burdock root, garlic, onions, parsley, rosemary, stinging nettle, thyme
Herbs for body and luster	Calendula, catnip, horsetail, licorice, lime flowers, nasturtium, parsley, rosemary, sage, stinging nettle, watercress
Herbs for shine	Horsetail, parsley, nettle, rosemary, sage, calendula
Herbs for hair growth	Aloe, arnica, birch, burdock, catmint, chamomile, horsetail, licorice, marigold, nettle, parsley, rosemary, sage, stinging nettle
Herbs for coloring	Brown: henna (reddish brown), walnut hulls, sage Blond: calendula, chamomile, lemon, saffron, turmeric, rhubarb root

Apple cider vinegar can be used as a conditioner or rinse and has all sorts of benefits for your scalp and hair. It helps to reduce frizz, prevent split ends, treat dry scalp (it has antibacterial and antifungal properties), balance pH, remove buildup, stimulate hair growth, detangle, and more!

Tropical Face Cleanser

The vitamin C in kiwi has enzymatic and cleansing properties, and the apricot oil serves as a moisturizer. The ground almonds act as an exfoliant to remove dead skin cells. Yogurt has cleansing and moisturizing properties.

Ingredients

1 kiwi
¾ cup avocado, banana, apricot, peach, strawberry, or papaya
  (or some of each)
2 tablespoons plain yogurt (whole milk is best)
1 tablespoon apricot oil (almond oil also works well)
1 tablespoon honey
1 teaspoon finely ground almonds

Directions

Puree all ingredients together. Massage into face and neck and rinse thoroughly with cool water. Store excess in refrigerator for 1 to 2 days.

Beneficial for Oily Skin	Beneficial for Normal Skin	Beneficial for Dry Skin
Lemons, grapes, limes, strawberries, grapefruits, apples	Peaches, papayas, tomatoes, apricots, bananas, persimmons, bell peppers, cucumbers, kiwis, pumpkins, watermelons	Carrots, iceberg lettuce, honeydew melons, avocados, cantaloupes

Coconut Oil Toothpaste

This recipe is incredibly simple to make, and by using it you'll avoid the fluoride, detergents, and chemicals found in many commercial toothpastes. Coconut oil is antibacterial, antifungal, and antimicrobial, and it helps to bind the other ingredients together into more of a paste than a powder. Baking soda is a cleanser, whitener, and mild abrasive. The essential oil makes the paste taste better and freshens your breath.

Ingredients
½ cup coconut oil
¼ cup baking soda
15 to 20 drops peppermint, cinnamon, or myrrh essential oil (or a combination)

Directions
If the coconut oil is hard, warm it slightly to soften. Stir in baking soda and essential oil and store in a small mason jar or other covered dish. To use, wet your toothbrush, dip it in the paste, and brush!

Household Cleansers and Detergents

Laundry Detergent

Making your own laundry detergent saves money and allows you to avoid the chemicals found in many commercial detergents. Dr. Bronner's bar soaps come in 5-ounce bars and Fels-Naptha bars are 5.5 ounces, so just use the whole bar—a little more or less will not make a noticeable difference in this recipe. All these ingredients can easily be purchased online.

Ingredients
1 (5- or 5.5-ounce) bar soap (Dr. Bronner's or Fels-Naptha is ideal)
1 cup borax
1 cup washing soda
20 drops lavender, lemon, jasmine, or geranium essential oil (optional)

Directions
Grate the soap in a food processor. Then switch to the blade attachment, add borax, washing soda, and essential oil (if using) and process until it becomes a fine powder. Store in a covered container and use 1 to 2 tablespoons of detergent per load of wash.

Reusable Dryer Sheets

Commercial dryer sheets are laden with chemicals, some of which (like alpha-terpineol and linalool) may cause nervous system disorders or are carcinogenic. So make your own reusable ones! The vinegar will help to soften the clothes and reduce static, and the essential oil will leave your laundry smelling however you want it to. Try using lavender, tea tree, or jasmine essential oil.

Ingredients
Cotton fabric
½ cup white vinegar, ideally organic
8 to 10 drops essential oil

Directions
Cut the fabric into four to six squares, each about 4 inches by 4 inches. Use pinking shears to help prevent fraying, or hem the edges if you're feeling ambitious. Or just don't worry about it—it's not that big a deal if your dryer sheets start to fray after a few loads. Combine the vinegar and essential oil in a glass jar with a tight-fitting lid. Place the fabric pieces inside, screw on the lid, and give the jar a shake. To use, take the squares out of the container, wring them out gently, and throw them in the dryer with your clothes. After the dryer is done, place the pieces back in the jar with the liquid until you're ready to do the next load.

Non-Toxic Window Cleaner

The cornstarch in this recipe helps to reduce streaks. Citrus essential oils are perfect, or you can skip the essential oils and add a tablespoon of lemon juice instead. Be sure to label the bottle when you're done.

Ingredients

¼ cup white or apple cider vinegar
¼ cup isopropyl (rubbing) alcohol
1 tablespoon cornstarch
1½ cups water
8 to 10 drops essential oil or 1 tablespoon lemon juice

Directions

Combine all ingredients in a spray bottle and shake. Label spray bottle with a permanent marker or with masking tape and a pen.

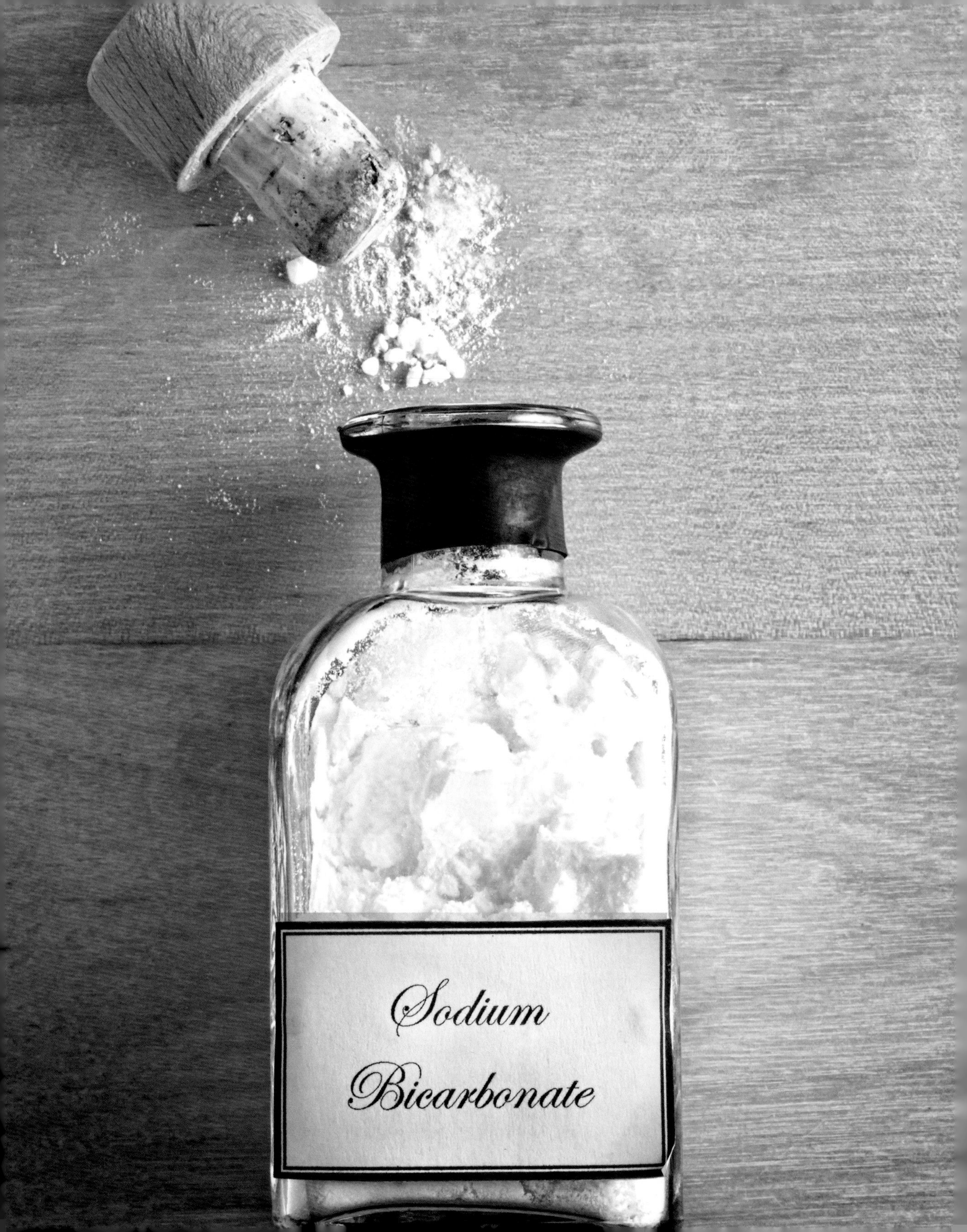
Sodium
Bicarbonate

DIY Bathroom Cleaner

This cleaner can be used for tiles, toilets, showers, or any other bathroom surface. Citrus, lavender, or tea tree essential oil is particularly nice in this recipe.

Ingredients
2 cups water
¼ cup white vinegar
1 tablespoon baking soda
1 tablespoon liquid castile soap
50 drops essential oil

Directions
Combine all ingredients in a spray bottle and shake. Label container. For tough stains or soap scum, spray on surface and allow to sit for several minutes before wiping off with a damp cloth.

Dish Soap

Use an all-natural bar soap for this recipe, since some bar soaps contain chemicals and artificial scents and dyes—Dr. Bronner's is always a good option. Super washing soda is inexpensive and can easily be found online. Citrus, lavender, or tea tree essential oil is ideal for this soap.

Ingredients
1¾ cups water
1 tablespoon super washing soda
1 tablespoon grated bar soap
15 to 20 drops essential oil

Directions
Heat water to boiling. In a heat-proof mixing bowl, combine super washing soda and grated bar soap. Pour boiling water over mixture and stir until smooth. Allow to sit for 6 to 8 hours, stirring occasionally, until soap gels. Add essential oil and mix. Use a funnel to pour into a bottle with a squirt top.

Super-Simple Kitchen Cleaner

For kitchen counters and stovetops, mix up ¼ cup baking soda with just enough water to form a paste. Dip your sponge in the paste and then scrub. So easy!

Furniture Polish

This mixture (affectionately known as "furniture salad dressing") will help clean, polish, and freshen your wooden furniture. Who knew salad dressing was so good for wood?

Ingredients
¾ cup olive oil
1 teaspoon flaxseed oil (optional)
¼ cup white vinegar
1 teaspoon lemon juice

Directions
Use a funnel to pour all ingredients into a squeeze bottle, and shake. Squeeze out a little onto a soft rag and rub into furniture. Oil and vinegar will separate, so always shake before using.

Index